# *Wittgenstein's Account of Truth*

SUNY series in Philosophy

George R. Lucas Jr., editor

# Wittgenstein's Account of Truth

Sara Ellenbogen

*State University of New York Press*

Published by
State University of New York Press, Albany

For information, address State University of New York Press,
90 State Street, Suite 700, Albany, NY 12207

Production by Judith Block
Marketing by Patrick Durocher

**Library of Congress Cataloging-in-Publication Data**

Ellenbogen, Sara.
    Wittgenstein's account of truth / Sara Ellenbogen.
       p.  cm. — (SUNY series in philosophy)
    Includes bibliographical references (p.) and index.
    ISBN 0-7914-5625-0 (alk. paper) — ISBN 0-7914-5626-9 (pbk. : alk. paper)
       1. Wittgenstein, Ludwig, 1889–1951. 2. Truth. I. Title. II. Series.

    B3376.W56.E52 2003
    121'.091—dc21                                                      2002067041

10 9 8 7 6 5 4 3 2 1

*For Ann and Lenny Feinzig*

"Knowledge is in the end based on acknowledgment."

—*On Certainty* #378

# Contents

# Abbreviations

B.B.        *The Blue and Brown Books*

P.I.        *Philosophical Investigations*

P.R.        *Philosophical Remarks*

O.C.        *On Certainty*

Z.          *Zettel*

# Preface

What does it mean to say that a statement is true? The traditional way of answering the question, which is known in philosophical circles as "realism," is that to say that a statement is true means that it corresponds to what it says. Yet there is the fact that we can make statements about states of affairs which we could not recognize. And then there is the fact that the word "true" has a use in our language; it may be said of a statement either correctly or incorrectly. So if it makes sense to say that there are conditions under which a statement should be called "true" or "false," it should be possible to explain how we could learn when we should call it "true" or "false." These considerations have inspired a view called semantic antirealism. The antirealist says that we cannot make sense of saying that a statement is true if the state of affairs which it asserts is one that we could not recognize. For if we cannot recognize what a statement asserts, we cannot learn the conditions under which we should call the statement "true."

Does it make sense to call a statement "true" if we cannot recognize what it asserts? This is the point at issue between the antirealist and the realist. But what has gone unnoticed is that the antirealist view that it does *not* make sense is premised on the realist assumption that what makes it correct to call a statement "true" is that it corresponds to how things are. For it is only on the assumption that what makes it correct to call a statement "true" is that the state of affairs asserted obtains that our inability to recognize a state of affairs is relevant to our ability to learn when we should call the statement "true." In other words, it will only seem to us that we cannot recognize the conditions under which we should call a statement "true" if we hold that those conditions are determined by its correspondence with how things are. If we were to revise our traditional view that what it means to call a statement "true" is that it corresponds with how things are, our inability to recognize a state of affairs would not be relevant to our ability to learn when we should call a statement "true." And it would no longer be obvious that it does not make sense to call a statement "true" or "false" if the state of affairs which it asserts transcends our recognitional capacities.

This work will show that the later Wittgenstein's conception of meaning does call for such a revision in our concept of what it means to call a statement "true." I argue that the dictum "meaning is use" implies that what makes it correct to call statements "true" is our agreement on the criteria whereby we call them "true." What it means, in our language, to call a statement "true" is that we judge it to be true, according to agreed-upon criteria of truth.

There will be objections to my reading of Wittgenstein. For Wittgenstein is often read as endorsing the deflationary view of truth, which holds that the content of "is true" is captured by the equivalence schema " 'p' is true if and only if p," or that to say that a statement is true is only another way of asserting it. The deflationist will not want to explicate the concept of truth in terms of another concept such as "criteria" because he thinks that all we can say about the nature of truth is that we use the truth predicate to express propositions. My view is not a rival interpretation of Wittgenstein but rather a drawing out of the implications of "meaning is use." Thus, I will not explicitly argue against the deflationist reading of Wittgenstein. But because the deflationist shares with me the assumption that our use of the word "true" is important for our concept of truth, I will explain where our views diverge.

According to the deflationary theory, as articulated by Paul Horwich, the function of the word "true" in sentences such as "p is true" is to make the assertion that would otherwise have to be made using another sentence expressing p. Thus, the predicate "is true" exists solely for the sake of our logical need to make assertions without employing or even knowing the sentences that express those assertions. For example, we sometimes want to assent to a proposition which we cannot name, as we do when we say "Whatever John says about it is true." Or again, sometimes we want to say something about an infinite set of propositions without enumerating them, such as "Everything that the pope says is true." The predicate "is true" thus allows us to express propositions which we cannot identify. What allows the notion of truth to play this role is the fact that for every declarative sentence "p," we are provided with an equivalent sentence, "the proposition that p is true." But, in Horwich's view, *nothing more about truth should be assumed.*

Horwich says that we are inclined to inflate the concept of truth because we falsely assimilate the truth predicate to other predicates. We are used to the fact that most predicates, such as "is magnetic," designate features of the world whose nature is revealed by investigation. And so we reason by analogy that the predicate "is true" must designate a feature of reality—truth—whose nature can be revealed by philosophical analysis. But the truth predicate is not like other predicates: it is not used to attribute to linguistic entities an ordinary sort of property. So Horwich holds that it is a mistake to think that truth has any underlying nature; in his view, there is no conception of truth to be had which goes beyond the triviality expressed by the equivalence schema. We cannot expect the truth predicate to participate in a theory of that to which it refers which specifies general conditions for our application of it.

What is correct about the deflationary view is its insistence that there is an unseverable link between asserting a statement and claiming it is true. We call a statement "true" when we want to affirm the statement. And the deflationist is right to assume that the concept of truth must pertain to language because the truth predicate is applied to what can be expressed in language.

Where I take issue with the deflationist is in his assumption that because "is true" is not used to attribute to linguistic entities an ordinary sort of property, we cannot specify the general conditions of our application of the predicate. It is this assumption which leads him to say that truth cannot be explicated by means of other concepts. And the assumption is false: granted, the truth predicate applies to linguistic entities, such as assertions. It does not follow that we can give no general account of the circumstances under which we apply the predicate, that is, under which we make assertions. We can surely say that we call statements "true" when and only when there is some normative way of establishing that they are true. And, if we take the spirit of Wittgenstein's conception of meaning seriously, then the fact that we use the word "true" under just these circumstances is relevant to what it means to apply the predicate and to what our concept of truth is.

That is to say: if we hold, with Wittgenstein, that meaning is use, then to ask about the meaning of a predicate such as "true" is to examine the rules and conventions which we take as making it correct for us to use it. So an inquiry into what it means to call a statement "true" must begin with the question, "What kinds of rules and conventions do we use in applying the truth predicate to statements?" Since we should have no way of knowing when to call a statement "true" if we could not, in principle, tell whether it was true, we call statements "true" or "false" when and only when we agree on criteria for determining whether they are true. Thus, what it means to call a statement "true" is that we have decided its truth.

Another way of putting this point is that if we are to explain the meaning of the word "true," we must construe what counts as using it correctly in a way which will allow us to explain how a speaker could learn what counts as using it correctly. As Wittgenstein points out in his private language argument, if the meaning of the word "pain" is taken as something which each person knows only from his own case rather than as the concept which we acquire through the language game of expressing pain, there is no way of explaining how a speaker could learn the public linguistic use of the word "pain." Consequently, there would be no way of explaining the meaning of the word "pain." As with the word "pain," so with the word "true": if what makes it correct to call statements "true" is not taken as something which we could recognize as making it correct to call them "true," there is no way of explaining how we could learn to use the word "true." And if there is no way of explaining how we can learn to use the word "true," then there is no way of explaining the meaning that the word "true" has in our language. Thus, what makes it correct to call a statement "true" cannot be its correspondence to *what* is asserted, where the state of affairs in question may transcend our recognitional capacities. Rather, the conditions under which it is correct to call a statement "true" are determined by the criterion whereby we judge its truth.

Wittgenstein's dictum "meaning is use" implies a robust account of truth, unlike those which are often attributed to him. In Wittgenstein's view, our concept of truth is internally related to our concept of knowledge, since we use the word "true" when we can confirm or disconfirm statements. So he would reject the thought that to call a statement "true" is merely to assert the statement. Rather, it is to make a claim about our epistemic position.

Nor would Wittgenstein endorse the antirealist view that we should revise our practice of calling certain statements "true" or "false." For that view is premised on a tacit realist assumption that what it means to call a statement "true" is that it corresponds to how things are. And if Wittgenstein is right, we should resist this picture: what it means to call a statement "true" is not that it corresponds to how things are, but that our criterion for accepting it is met. If we revise our view of what it means to call a statement "true," we will not need to stop treating certain statements as true or false. We will merely stop using the word "true" in the realist sense. Henceforth, when we say that a statement is true we will take ourselves to mean that we deem ourselves correct in asserting it on the basis of the criteria which we currently treat as decisive.

# Acknowledgments

This book was originally written as a doctoral dissertation at the University of Toronto under the direction of two generous and conscientious supervisors, Cheryl Misak and Peter Apostoli. I am also grateful to my reader, Stuart Shanker at York University, for his helpful comments and warm encouragement. Carol Caraway read and commented on an entire draft of the manuscript, for which I am very grateful. I have also been helped by discussions with Peter Baumann and Winston Langley.

I thank Suma Rajiva, Zahra Merali, Sharon Kaye, Wendy LeMarquand, and Clare Pain for their friendship and support while I was completing the project. And last, but not least, I thank my undergraduate professors at the University of Massachusetts at Boston—particularly Robert Shope and Nelson Lande—for their fine instruction and early encouragement.

# From "Meaning is Use" to the Rejection of Transcendent Truth

The later Wittgenstein's conception of meaning as use is often taken as providing the inspiration for semantic antirealism. That is, it is taken as having inspired the view put forth by Michael Dummett and Crispin Wright in the 1980s that we should reject a theory of meaning that is based on truth conditions in favor of one based on assertibility conditions. Yet, by rejecting truth conditions, antirealists such as Dummett go much further than Wittgenstein. For, as I will argue, to hold that because Wittgenstein rejected realism he therefore must be an antirealist is to fail to recognize that Wittgenstein held a unique account of truth which does not fit neatly into the categories of realism and antirealism and which, moreover, undermines the dichotomy between them. Wittgenstein did not reject the idea that sentences have truth conditions. Rather, he revised his conception of a truth condition. He held that truth conditions are determined by criteria, that is, by conventional rules which tell us the circumstances under which it is correct to predicate "is true" of our statements. And he argued that, as statements within different language games are accepted as true upon different kinds of grounds, the kind of certainty that we require in order to accept a sentence as true depends on the language game to which the statement belongs. Therefore, Wittgenstein has a unique conception of truth which can be applied, across the board, to all sentences in language; a conception which links the truth condition of every type of sentence which is treated as being true or false to the way that the sentence is used.

1

I shall first outline the positive account of truth that falls out of the dictum that meaning is use. I shall then argue that the antirealist's case for replacing truth conditions with assertibility conditions presupposes a realist conception of truth which Wittgenstein explicitly rejected. Finally, I shall show how Wittgenstein's account of truth avoids the objections which can be made against both realism and antirealism. For through his more radical break with the realist/correspondence view, he puts forth an account of truth that avoids the truth value gaps that prompt the antirealist to reject truth conditions.

## 1. Wittgenstein's Rejection of Realism versus Semantic Antirealism

Wittgenstein's rejection of a realist conception of meaning in favor of his account of meaning as use led to his parallel rejection of a realist picture of truth which holds that propositions are true by virtue of their correspondence to facts which might transcend our capacity for knowledge. For Wittgenstein reasoned that as there is nothing more to meaning than use, there is nothing more to our concept of truth than we can grasp through our use of statements which we treat, in our language, as being true or false. In Wittgenstein's view, it only makes sense to think of truth in terms of our capacity for knowledge. For we acquire the concept of truth by learning how to apply the predicate "is true" to statements in our language, that is, by learning what counts as establishing our statements as true. And we learn what counts as establishing statements as true by participating in the linguistic practices of a community. For just as within a linguistic community we agree on correct uses of words, we also agree upon methods of testing the statements which we treat as being true or false. That is to say, as we participate together in the rule-following practices within a community, we play various kinds of language games and engage in various kinds of inquiry.[1] In each type of inquiry, we devise methods of testing assertions which are appropriate tests of statements within that type of language game. We agree on what is to count as an adequate test of any given type of statement. And thus we agree on criteria which determine when it is correct to predicate "is true" of sentences within each type of language game. Therefore, an individual who has mastered a language has acquired the concept of how to establish something as true. For as he is initiated into the linguistic practices of a community, he learns conventional rules for predicating "is true" of the sentences in language which his community treats as being true or false.[2] Wittgenstein remarks,

> What counts as [a] test [of a statement]?—"But is this an adequate test? . . ."—As if giving grounds did not come to an end sometime. But the end is not an ungrounded presupposition: it is an ungrounded way of acting. (*O.C.* #110)

Wittgenstein's contention here is that if we want to know why the ground on which we accept a particular statement is an adequate ground upon which to claim to know that it is true, we cannot hope to find the answer by looking further than the language game in which the statement is used. For there is no extralinguistic standard by reference to which we could assess the adequacy of our methods of testing our statements. Thus, just as nothing determines the meanings of words other than the rules of a linguistic community for the correct and incorrect ways of using them, nothing determines the circumstances under which it is correct to predicate "is true" of a sentence other than our agreement on the conventional rules whereby we predicate "is true" of our sentences. That is, nothing determines the conditions under which we are *correct* in predicating "is true" of a sentence other than a rule of language which tells us the grounds upon which we may accept it as true.

When Wittgenstein rejected a realist account of truth, he conceived of questions about truth in terms of questions about meaning. He held that it is only within a language in which human beings agree on conventions for predicating "is true" of their statements that statements can be said to be true or false. For it is only within a form of life—that is, within the world picture to which the language we speak commits us—that there are grounds for affirming and denying statements. He does not want to say that human agreement decides what is true and false. Instead, he holds that human agreement provides the framework within which it makes sense to speak of truth and falsehood. For "true" and "false" are linguistic predicates, that is, they apply exclusively to statements. And if there were no agreement on how to apply these predicates, then the context in which they have meaning would not exist. Thus, rather than saying that human agreement decides what is true and false, it would be more accurate to say that human agreement creates the conditions under which it is *correct* for us to predicate "is true" and "is false" of our statements. But the notion of correctness being invoked here does not correspond to what we usually think of as making it correct to predicate "is true" of a statement—i.e., that the statement corresponds to the way things are. On a conception of meaning as use, what makes it correct for us to call statements "true" are the linguistic rules whereby we apply the predicate to statements in our language. These rules and conventions are based upon our conceptual system. Consequently, they can be revised when our conceptual system changes. Thus, Wittgenstein remarks, "It is what human beings *say* that is true or false and they agree on the language they use. That is not agreement in opinions but in form of life" (*P.I.* #241).

Agreement in form of life is logically prior to agreement in opinions. For agreement in form of life is our agreement on a shared world picture. And this world picture forms the inherited background against which we distinguish between true and false (*O.C.* #94). Or, to put the point another way, agreement in form of life is our agreement on a set of grammatical propositions or "hinge propositions" which, among other things, describe what counts as compelling grounds for certainty of statements within our different language games (cf. *O.C.* #270, #271). Thus, agreement in form of life is what grounds our ability to communicate and to argue and inquire. It provides the framework within which agreement in opinions may or may not take place.[3] The form of life *within which* a community's statements count as true or false cannot itself be tested for correctness.[4] For the set of hinge propositions which we accept as true forms our basis for making judgments. And, as Wittgenstein remarks, "If [we] want the door to turn, the hinges must stay put" (*O.C.* #343)—that is, we may not call into question the totality of statements that our community accepts as true at once if we are to continue to judge. A form of life within which hypotheses can be tested and answers given cannot be called into question all at once from within that form of life because it is the very framework within which questions can be framed (*O.C.* #205). It is the framework within which human beings are able to form and express beliefs and make assertions. Therefore, it is also the framework within which they devise methods of testing beliefs and assertions. As Wittgenstein notes,

> We call something a proposition when *in our language* we apply the calculus of truth functions to it. And the use of the words "true" and "false" may be among the constituent parts of the game, and, if so, it belongs to our concept 'proposition,' but does not fit it. (*P.I.* #136)

For the realist who holds that we can conceive of the truth of a statement independently of our practice of calling it true, the truth of a sentence is independent of our capacity for knowledge. But for Wittgenstein, who holds that the predicate "is true" applies only to sentences in language for which we have ways of determining their truth, truth is wholly a function of our capacity for knowledge. Since the meaning of a proposition is determined by the conditions for knowledge as laid down by our conventions of testing, truth cannot be conceived of as independent of our capacity for knowledge.[5]

Wittgenstein's rejection of a realist picture of truth has been taken as semantic antirealism by Michael Dummett and Crispin Wright in the 1980s. Semantic antirealism, in its simplest terms, is the view that knowledge of the truth conditions of sentences in a language is not what we as language speakers acquire when we come to understand that language.[6] Instead, we learn the conditions under which we are justified in asserting the sentences in language which we treat as being true or false. The argument for antirealism is that some sentences which we treat as being true or false, or bivalent, would have truth conditions transcending our ability to recognize them, for the process of verifying such sentences would outrun our ability to learn of their truth value. Statements about the remote past, for example, are held by the antirealist not to be determinately true or false, because in order to know what would render such statements true or false, we would have to be able to survey the past as we do the present. Clearly, there often is nothing left of the past, and so we are unable to do so. Antirealists hold that our linguistic practice of treating such statements as determinately true or false is inaccurate and in need of revision. They argue that since we cannot have learned how to use these sentences by learning to recognize their truth conditions as obtaining when they obtain, we cannot give a truth-conditional account of their meaning, but only one in terms of the conditions which justify asserting them.

I will examine the argument for attributing this form of antirealism to Wittgenstein in part II. But for now it is important to see that Wittgenstein's rejection of a realist/correspondence account of truth is more radical than the antirealist's. The antirealist is still, in a sense, committed to the correspondence theory of truth even while he rejects the possibility of giving a truth-conditional account of meaning. That is, he implicitly assumes that the only viable account of truth would have to be a realist account. Thus, he accepts the realist view that the truth of statements about the remote past must consist of their correspondence with that particular segment of reality of which there now no longer exists any evidence. And it is his commitment to this correspondence account of truth that forces him to deny that such statements have truth conditions after he has rejected the idea of transcendent truth, that is, after he has insisted that if something is true, it must be possible for us to know that it is true. For his belief in the correspondence theory of what makes statements about the past true causes an antirealist to hold that finding out whether they are true must involve surveying the past as we do the present. But his agreement with Wittgenstein's verificationist thought that if something is true, it must be possible for us to know that it is true, makes the antirealist say that since we cannot discover whether statements about the past are true, such statements do not have truth conditions. Thus, the antirealist denies that statements about the past have truth conditions because the only kind of truth conditions he recognizes are realist truth conditions, and when these are undermined by verificationist scruples, he has nothing left to replace them with.

Wittgenstein's rejection of a realist account of truth goes further than antirealism. For while Wittgenstein shares with antirealists the thought that if something is true it must be possible for us to know that it is true, he does not share their commitment to the realist doctrine that the truth of a statement about the past must consist in its correspondence with some segment of reality in virtue of which it is true. Thus, Wittgenstein is not forced to deny that statements about the past have truth conditions because, unlike the antirealist, he has an alternative conception of a truth condition with which to replace realist truth conditions.

## 2. *The Positive Account of Truth*

Wittgenstein holds that truth conditions are determined by criteria, that is, by rules which determine, by linguistic convention, the circumstances under which we may predicate "is true" of the sentences in language which we treat as being true or false. For, according to Wittgenstein, every type of statement to which we apply the predicates "is true" and "is false" is governed by some criterion for determining its truth value. As he remarks, "Really, 'The proposition is either true or false' only means that it must be possible to decide for or against it. But this does not say what the ground for such a decision is like" (*O.C.* #200).

In other words, whenever we treat a statement as being true or false in our language, we consider something or other to be an adequate test of a statement of that kind. To say that a statement is either true or false is to say that we have some criterion for determining its truth value; that we treat something as being decisive for establishing the statement as true and, thus, as being an adequate ground upon which to affirm that statement.[1] And because different kinds of statements are accepted as true upon different kinds of grounds, if we want to know what our ground for affirming a particular statement is like, we must examine the language game in which the statement is used.

Criterial rules tell us, as part of the "logic" or grammar of the language games in which we apply them, what count as adequate tests of the kinds of statements that we make within these language games. For example, if our criterion for ascribing pain to someone is met—that is, if someone says that she is in pain and if questions about her truthfulness do not arise—then it is correct to affirm that she is in pain. It is a misdescription of our practice of making pain ascriptions to say that we cannot know but can only guess that another person is in pain because we do not, in *real* cases, doubt that others are in pain (*P.I.* #303). The reason we do not treat our inability to feel someone else's pain as relevant to whether we can know that she is in pain is that we learn the *concept* of another's pain when we learn language—that is, when we learn how to use sentences such as "He is in pain" and "She is in pain." And the language game in which we learn to make third-person pain ascriptions begins with the *expression* of pain since, obviously, it is a background condition of our practice that we cannot feel someone else's sensation of pain (*P.I.* #288). Because the background condition of our practice of making pain ascriptions places limits on what can count as evidence for statements within this language game, what we treat as establishing them as true differs from what we treat as establishing the truth value of statements within other types of language games. And, consequently, what makes it correct to predicate "is true" of statements within one language game is different from what makes it correct to predicate "is true" of statements within another language game. What counts as an adequate test of one type of statement cannot be the standard of what should count as an adequate test of another type of statement since the various kinds of statements that we treat as being true or false do not all admit of the same kind of verification. Furthermore, we have different needs and purposes in classifying our different statements as true or false, and these purposes partly determine what we are willing to treat as decisively establishing the truth value of a given kind of statement. Therefore, the kinds of criteria whereby we determine the truth values of our statements vary across our different language games according to the background conditions of our practices and our purposes in treating statements as true or false.

In some of our language games, the criteria governing our statements take the form of tests by which we judge that something is the case, which become the conventional standards by reference to which we justify our judgments. In Wittgenstein's example, if medical science discovers that angina is caused by a certain bacillus, then to answer the question, "How do you know this man has angina?" by saying "I have found the bacillus in his blood" is to state the criterion of angina—that is, it is a loose way of defining angina. By contrast, to reply to the question "How do you know he has angina?" by citing the presence of a symptom of the condition which has been found in some way to coincide with our defining criterion is to make a hypothesis rather than to decisively justify the judgment (*B.B.*, p. 24).

In language games in which we have no way of distinguishing criteria from symptoms in a way that is not ad hoc, our criteria take the form of defining characteristics of an object or a condition, where the presence of these characteristics is decisive for establishing the existence of the thing in question. For example, in answer to the question, "How do you know that it is a diamond?" a jeweler might cite the physical properties of a stone that establish that it is a diamond. In a looser, derivative sense of the word "criterion," we could speak of the criterion of being an orange as the way an orange looks, tastes, and smells. And a speaker could justify the judgment "This is an orange" by citing the presence of these features. For these features constitute ways of telling, and language users take them as settling the truth of judgments.[2]

The one exception to the generalization that every type of statement which we treat as being true or false is governed by a criterion for determining its truth value is the first-person avowal "I am in pain." "I am in pain" can be either true or false since one can lie about being in pain. But it is a mistake to think of this statement as an assertion which the speaker himself could justify or determine by reference to a criterion. For there is no way that a speaker could verify or *come to know* that he was in pain. That is, there is no way that a speaker could pass through a state of not knowing that he was in pain to knowing it. Thus, the statement "I am in pain" does not express a speaker's *judgment* that he is in pain. And because this statement does not express a judgment, it is not governed by a criterion.

By contrast, whenever we make judgments and assertions, we employ criteria by reference to which we justify our assertions. For an essential feature of criteria is that they can be cited in response to the question "How do you know that such and such is the case?" Criteria provide the grounds whereby we justify our judgments by describing what counts as settling the truth of particular types of statements.

Statements of criterial rules determine the truth conditions of our statements because they state grammatical truths or conceptually necessary statements. That is to say, it is true in virtue of a rule of language, convention, or definition that if a certain bacillus is found in someone's blood, that person has angina. Thus, as long as this bacillus remains our criterion of having angina, it is not logically possible that the bacillus should be present and the criterially governed object (angina) absent. Or, to take another example, it is not logically possible for our criterion for saying that someone is in pain to be met and for that person not to be in pain.[3] For criteria determine, as part of the grammar or logic of a statement that some state of affairs obtains, the circumstances under which it is correct to affirm the statement. They define what it means to call something true within a particular language game. Therefore, it is not possible for the criterion of a claim to be met and for the criterially governed claim to be false, for this would violate a rule of language.

Criteria differ from realist truth conditions in that a conventional rule for predicating "is true" of a sentence is always linked to the way in which we currently use a sentence. For another way of putting the point that truth conditions are determined by criteria is to say that truth conditions are determined by our current ways of determining our statements' truth values. And, of course, the consequence of the view that the truth condition of a statement is determined by our current way of telling whether it is true is that the truth condition of any given statement must be internally related to our current capacity for knowledge. For the standards by which we judge whether something is true reflect what we know at a particular time. What we accept as an adequate ground on which to accept a statement as true reflects the current state of our knowledge. And, obviously, the grounds upon which we accept our statements as true can change in response to empirical discoveries.

What we currently take to be a defining characteristic of some state of affairs which is decisive for establishing that it obtains can subsequently be discovered to be merely contingently associated with it (*P.I.* #354; *B.B.*, pp. 24–25; *Z.* #438). That is, there can be a fluctuation between criteria and symptoms. For example, from the beginning of the seventeenth to the late nineteenth century, the defining criterion of gold was solubility in aqua regia. But in the nineteenth century it was discovered that gold had the atomic number 79, *a feature not exclusively correlated* with the feature of solubility in aqua regia; that is, the former criterion was discovered to have room for non-"noble" metals whereas the latter criterion uniquely defined "gold." Thus, with the discovery of the atomic number of gold, the old criterion was downgraded to symptom status.[4] We can also simply discover that we were wrong about what we previously held as true; we were not yet aware of any countervailing factors which would have cast doubt upon our ways of judging (*O.C.* #124). Therefore, the conventions according to which it is correct to predicate "is true" of our statements are subject to revision as our knowledge increases. As Wittgenstein remarks, our language games change with time (*O.C.* #256). What gets treated one day as a proposition to be tested by experience may get treated another day as a rule of testing (*O.C.* #198; cf. *O.C.* #63, #65; *Z.* #352). And, conversely, propositions which were treated as norms of description can come to lose that status. For example, the statements "It is impossible to get to the moon," "Lightning never strikes in the same place twice," and perhaps "The earth is flat" were accepted as true by previous groups of inquirers, but they are not held true today. The thrust of identifying truth conditions with criteria or conventional rules is that the Wittgensteinian wants to say that previous inquirers were *correct* to say "It's true that lightning never strikes in the same place twice," and so forth, although it would now be incorrect to predicate "is true" of those sentences (*O.C.* #542, #607, #124, #191).

Those with realist sympathies will resist saying that our criteria determine the conditions under which it is correct to predicate "is true" of our statements. They will argue that if we turn out to be wrong about what we held true, we will not have been correct to predicate "is true" of a statement asserting it. For, according to any type of realist, what makes it correct to predicate "is true" of a statement is something other than the fact that our current criterion for calling it true is met. For example, the correspondence theorist will say that it is correct to predicate "is true" of a statement only if it corresponds with the way things are. And the internal realist or pragmatist will say that it is correct to predicate "is true" of a statement only if that statement should happen to be one that would still be believed if inquiry were to be pursued as far as it could fruitfully go.[5] And according to either of these conceptions of what makes our applications of "is true" correct, if it is incorrect for us to predicate "is true" of a statement on a certain basis now, it was incorrect for us to apply the truth predicate to that statement earlier, even if it was rationally acceptable to refer to that basis at the time.

The Wittgensteinian reply to the realist is that, if it is not to be a mystery how we can learn the meaning of "is true," we need to jettison the notion that what makes our applications of "is true" correct is something that could transcend our current knowledge. For by espousing an account of what constitutes a correct use of "is true," which makes the correctness of our applications of the predicate depend upon something which can outrun our current knowledge, we are attempting to attach a meaning to "is true" which outruns the use to which we can put the predicate. If we are to be able to give an account of the meaning which "is true" has in *our* language, it must be possible to explain how we could learn to use "is true" correctly. And it can only be possible to explain how we can learn to use "is true" correctly if what makes our applications of "is true" correct is taken as something which we could *recognize* as making them correct. Therefore, what makes our applications of "is true" correct must be something within the current scope of our knowledge. In other words, our applications of "is true" can only be made correct by the criteria that we currently accept as adequate tests of our statements. And these criteria can only be based upon the current state of our knowledge.

Furthermore, it is a feature of the growth of knowledge that there is never a point at which we can say that the statements which we currently hold as true are no longer open to revision, for our epistemic perspective on the growth of knowledge is limited by our being temporally located at a discrete point in the course of human inquiry. This limit forces us to say, with Wittgenstein, that "sure evidence is what we *accept* as sure" (*O.C.* #196). That is, it only makes sense to *call* sure evidence "evidence that we currently accept as sure." For we have no way of knowing what evidence *will be* held sure in the future. As Hilary Putnam has pointed out, statements which were rationally acceptable before are no longer rationally acceptable. And, for all we know, the criteria whereby we currently judge statements to be true or false will not be the same criteria whereby future generations will predicate "is true" and "is false" of their statements. So the Wittgensteinian will argue that if truth is one of *our* concepts, then the meaning of "is true" must be taken as being determined by *our* criteria for applying the predicate to particular statements in our current linguistic practices. The criteria whereby we apply the truth predicate reflect the state of our knowledge at a particular time. Therefore, what makes it correct to predicate "is true" of a statement must be internally related to our current capacity for knowledge.

Another way of putting this point is that what makes it correct to predicate "is true" of a statement cannot outrun what we know at a given time, and thus what we can assert. For unlike other predicates which apply to that which can be conceived independently of our linguistic practices, "is true" applies exclusively to bits of language such as beliefs, statements, and assertions. Hence, the concept of "a truth" is equivalent to the concept of a true belief, statement, or assertion. As Donald Davidson remarks, without creatures using sentences, the concept of truth would have no application.[6] And this is why we cannot explain the concept of truth without reference to human agreement on how to classify assertions as true. For an assertion is something that has a use within a language; it is something that we want to say can be made correctly or incorrectly. And we could not give content to saying that a speaker had asserted something correctly or incorrectly if we did not agree on what counts as a proper basis upon which to make an assertion. For here we should have no criterion for saying that someone had asserted something correctly (cf. *P.I.* #199, #202, #258, #265). That is, it is a property of assertions that we do employ criteria which tell us when it is correct to make them. So an assertion for which we had no such criterion could not play a role in any of our language games. Therefore, what makes it correct to make an assertion—and hence to apply the truth predicate to an assertion—can only be construed in terms of our agreement on how to classify an assertion as true. Thus, when we change our ways of judging our statements' truth values, we change the conditions under which it is correct to call our statements "true."

It follows that truth is not a use-independent property of a statement. Nor is truth a relation between a thought or a statement and a mind- or language-independent item like a fact. The predicates "is true" and "is false" do not apply to facts, but to what is said. And what is said is not like what is eaten, for instance, a cake. The word "what" in the phrase "what is said" does not name an object. Instead, it introduces a propositional clause or a "that" clause. It introduces a belief or an assertion which gets expressed in language by a thinking creature.[7] And what determines the conditions under which it is correct to make an assertion is our normative agreement, *here and now*, on what count as adequate grounds *upon which* to affirm a statement (*O.C.* #270, #271, #200, #82). For it is a background condition of our practice of applying the truth predicate that we cannot foresee our acquisition of any information which would make it incorrect for us to apply "is true" to our statements, even though we know that it is theoretically possible that we may acquire such information. Therefore, the fact that previous communities held as true statements like "Lightning never strikes in the same place twice," and so forth, made it *correct* to predicate "is true" of those sentences, although it did *not* make it correct to predicate "is true" of them *come what may*.

That is, it did not make it correct to predicate "is true" of them in the light of future discoveries or recalcitrant experience. Rather, our empirical discoveries caused us to revise the conditions under which we were willing to predicate "is true" of these sentences of which we previously had been objectively certain (Z. #352).[8] But nevertheless, before we were forced to revise our ways of judging the truth values of these sentences, that is, before we revised our conventions for predicating "is true" of them, it was *correct* to predicate "is true" of them. For although we must revise our application of "is true" to sentences when we find we can no longer take them as true, there is no other use which "is true" could have in our language—there is no other way in which it would be correct to use it—except as a predicate which we apply to whatever we *now* take true. As Wittgenstein puts this point,

> Well if everything speaks for an hypothesis and nothing speaks against it—is it certainly true? One may designate it as such.— But does it agree with reality, with the facts?—With this question, you are already going round in a circle. (*O.C.* #191)

Wittgenstein's point here is that no new information is gained by asking whether a statement which we *designate* as true agrees with reality or with the facts. For the concepts of truth and falsity cannot be explained without reference to our practice of *calling* statements true (*P.I.* #136). Nor, therefore, can they be explained without reference to our agreement on the standards by which we judge statements as true and the grounds upon which we accept them as true: "The reason why the use of the expression 'true or false' has something misleading about it is that it is like saying 'it tallies with the facts or it doesn't,' and the very thing that is in question is what 'tallying' is here" (*O.C.* #199). That is: we may conceivably revise our world picture so that today's propositions will not seem to tally with what we will then take as "the facts." But this possibility plays no role in our practice of *treating* statements as true or false or acting *as though* they were true or false (*O.C.* #110, #652, #342, #341, #343). What determines the correct uses of "is true" can only be our agreement, within a community, on the conventions and criteria whereby we apply the predicate to statements. So to ask whether we are correct to predicate "is true" of a statement will only be a question about what our practice actually is, rather than a query about whether this practice is actually justified by reference to some extralinguistic standard which is informed by facts that transcend our current knowledge.[9]

Therefore, to paraphrase an argument of Hans-Johann Glock's, to express the fact that the way things are is independent of what we say about it by saying "Before 1900, there was a truth that there were radioactive substances" is infelicitous. And so is the even more acceptable "It was true before 1900 that there were radioactive substances." What can be said is "It is true that before 1900 there were radioactive substances." And this is logically equivalent to "There were radioactive substances before 1900." That this was so independently of our thinking so has nothing to do with the mind-independent nature of truth nor with the alleged eternal existence of an abstract realm in which truths subsist. It has everything to do with the fact that our saying that p doesn't make it the case that p. Our conception of truth as objective—that is, as not being dependent on what anyone says or thinks—arises from our awareness that "People say that p" and "p" do not entail each other.[10] The conditions under which we are correct to predicate "is true" of a statement at a given time and the conditions under which the statement corresponds to reality can come apart. We recognize that they can come apart. And we use "is true" as though these conditions do come apart in our practice of affirming or asserting our statements. We do not take the fact that we currently predicate "is true" of any given sentence as making it correct to continue to predicate "is true" of it *come what may*. We predicate "is true" of our sentences knowing full well that it is theoretically conceivable that they may have to be withdrawn (*O.C.* #620, #652). And when we find out that we were wrong about something, we are willing to revise our practice of applying the truth predicate to a given statement. But although we hold in such a case that we were wrong *about* what we asserted, we do not say that we were wrong to *predicate* "is true" of our statement at the time when we made it. We do not say this any more than one would say that one was wrong to say "I know that N.N. will arrive in half an hour's time," when one has spoken to N.N. ten minutes ago on the telephone, even if N.N. gets into an accident after calling and never does arrive. In such a situation, we would have to say that we didn't *actually* know, but only thought we knew. But it would be misleading to say that someone had not been right to *say* "I know" in a context in which his or her knowledge claim had been justified merely because the content of the claim had actually been false (*O.C.* #542).

By parity of reasoning, it is incoherent to say that we were incorrect to apply the truth predicate to a statement that we were once justified in accepting merely because the statement has since been falsified and revised. For, as we saw in the first chapter, if we did not treat the statements that we are currently justified in accepting *as though* they were true *in spite* of our knowing that any of them may be revised, we would not have a framework within which we could conceive of possible recalcitrant experiences.[11] Hence, we would not have a framework within which to classify beliefs as true or false, for we would not have a framework within which to judge. As Wittgenstein puts this point,

> if you tried to doubt everything, you would not get as far as doubting anything. The game of doubting itself presupposes certainty (O.C. #115). All testing . . . and disconfirmation of a hypothesis takes place already within a system. And this system is . . . the element in which arguments have their life. (*O.C.* #105)

Therefore, insofar as our practice requires us to treat the statements that we are currently justified in accepting as true, we have to say that we were *correct* to treat a statement that we have revised as true at the time when we were justified in accepting it. And once we grant that we were correct to treat a statement *as though* it were true, it is unclear what it would mean to say that we were not correct to *call* it true. As Wittgenstein remarks, "A judge might even say 'That is the truth—so far as a human being can know it.' But what would this rider achieve? ('beyond all reasonable doubt')" (*O.C.* #607).

The fact that we revise the conditions under which we apply the truth predicate to particular statements does not mean that "is true" applies to what is independent of our current knowledge. For "is true" is a word which is used to predicate something of beliefs. Its meaning—which, on a Wittgensteinian view, boils down to its correct use—depends on our normative agreement on how we are to apply it in particular cases. The conditions under which it is correct to predicate "is true" of a sentence depend on our agreement on how the predicate is to be applied to a particular kind of sentence. They depend on our agreement on what counts as an adequate test of a particular kind of statement, that is, of a statement within a particular kind of language game (*O.C.* #82). This means that the predicate "is true" can only be meaningfully applied to a sentence for which we have some criterion or some convention whereby we predicate "is true" or "is false" of it. We cannot give content to calling something true where we have no criterion for determining its truth or falsehood.

Hans-Johann Glock would take issue with the last thought that I have expressed because he thinks that truths can exist without people. According to Glock, if there were no people, it would still be a truth that there are mountains. For, as he argues,

1. "If there were no people, there would still be mountains"

implies

> 2. "If there were no people, it would still be true that there are mountains,"

which in turn seems to imply

> 3. "If there were no people, it would still be a truth that there are mountains."

Richard Rorty has recently objected to the move from the first statement to the second by asking, "What is 'be true' supposed to mean in a world in which there are no statements to be true nor minds to have true beliefs?"[12] According to Rorty, the realist cannot reply to this question without dogmatically presupposing his account of truth. Glock argues that Rorty's conclusion is precipitous because it runs together the question of what "is true" means *in* a world without people with what it means *of* a world without people: "[the fact that] in a world without people, no one would be in a position to explain the meaning of 'is true' or use it in statements like (2) does not entail that *we* cannot meaningfully use 'is true' to make a statement like (2)." However, Glock's reasoning here is inconsistent with his other claim that "It was true before 1900 that there were radioactive substances" is infelicitous. For the reason that this statement is infelicitous is that *in that time* there was no such truth. The reason that *we* can say "It's true that there were radioactive substances before 1900" is that we can formulate that proposition *now*. Therefore, if Glock wants to claim that the counterfactual "If there were no people it would still be true that there are mountains" is a claim about what "is true" means *of* a world without people, then he owes us an account of why he gives the temporal adverb "Before 1900" an "in" reading while he gives the counterfactual adverb "If there were no people" an "of" reading, given that both types of adverbs are sentential operators. For, from the point of view of modal logic, the "in/of" distinction is a scope distinction. And scope distinctions are purely formal. Grammatically and formally, all sentential operators play the same role.[13]

Moreover, we do not need to invoke the "in/of" distinction to show that the claim "If there were no people it would still be a truth that there are mountains" is a claim about what "is true" means *in* a world without people. We need not use the language of modal logic to show that the realist cannot reply to the question "What is 'be true' supposed to mean in a world in which there are no minds to have true beliefs?" without dogmatically presupposing his own account of truth.

We need only ask, "What is the word *'it'* supposed to refer to in the sentence, "If there were no people, *it* would still be true that there are mountains"? It must surely refer to some bit of language, such as a belief or an assertion. For even if this sentence is paraphrased as "If there were no people, *that* there are mountains would still be true," we are still left with a counterfactual adverb modifying a that-clause. And a that-clause introduces a propositional attitude such as a belief. Now we can ask, In virtue of *what* could such a belief or assertion be true? In virtue of what would it be *correct* to predicate "is true" of "There are mountains"? In virtue of which standards of classification would some things count as mountains? Of course, what we call mountains would still exist, but if there were no intersubjective agreement on what counts as a mountain, what would make it correct to predicate "is true" of "there are mountains"? And if nothing could make it correct to predicate "is true" of "there are mountains," then in virtue of what would it be true? In virtue of what *could* it be true other than in virtue of that statement's correspondence with a fact—specifically, with the fact that *what* we call mountains would still exist in the absence of human conceptualization and classification? And if the realist were to give this answer, then he would, as Rorty says, be dogmatically presupposing his account of truth. For, as P. M. S. Hacker points out, on a Wittgensteinian view, what is true or false is what is believed, and what is believed are not *sentences*, but what is expressed by their use.[14] So in a world in which there was no use of language, there would be nothing that would be true or false. My point here goes beyond Donald Davidson's observation and Cheryl Misak's observation that if there were no beliefs for the truth predicate to apply to, truth would be "an uninstantiated property."[15] The problem lies deeper than that: if there were no speakers, there would be no intersubjective agreement *in virtue of which* beliefs and assertions could be true. And, thus, I think we can say: although the conditions under which something is *real* or is the case are independent of our normative agreement, the conditions under which it is correct to predicate "is true" of a sentence are wholly dependent on our normative agreement. These conditions are dependent on our agreement on what count as adequate grounds upon which to affirm our statements (*O.C.* #82, #270, #271). And the grounds which we consider to be telling or adequate on which to accept our statements as true can only reflect the state of our knowledge at a particular time.

We see, therefore, how Wittgenstein's conception of meaning as use implies the rejection of a realist account of truth. His conception of the truth condition of a sentence in terms of a convention for predicating "is true" of it or a conventionally accepted way of telling whether it is true entails the rejection of any view whereby truth can transcend our current capacity for knowledge. The realist objects to saying that truth conditions are determined by our current criteria for determining truth values because of his concern about yet-to-be-discovered facts. For he holds that if we could turn out to be wrong about what we previously held to be true, then the view that criteria determine truth conditions amounts to a kind of idealism. That is, it amounts to the view that the way things are is a product of our thought and talk. We have seen how Wittgenstein can avoid this charge of idealism by distinguishing the grammar of "is real" from the grammar of "is true."

The antirealist, as we shall see, also takes issue with the view that criteria determine truth conditions. For while he agrees with Wittgenstein's thought that truth cannot transcend our capacity for knowledge, he is also committed to the realist conception of truth as correspondence with reality. This places him in a dilemma about what to say about yet-to-be-discovered or undiscoverable facts given his prior commitment to the view of truth as correspondence and his subsequent rejection of the notion of transcendent truth. He attempts to relieve the tension in the following way: he holds that given that there *are* undiscovered facts and given that truth cannot transcend our capacity for knowledge, we should simply jettison the concept of truth and replace it with that of assertibility.[16]

Wittgenstein holds that the antirealist's move ought to be resisted (*O.C.* #607). For the fact is that we *use* the predicate "is true" to indicate that we are basing a claim we are making on our current norms of verification. We have a picture of truth as correspondence because of our awareness of the fact that "We say that p" does not entail "p." That is, we picture truth as correspondence because we know that the fact that we call a statement true does not necessarily mean that it will be correct to call it true in the future. This gives us a strong inclination to think of the truth conditions of our statements as being stable and determinate. We feel that what *makes* it correct to predicate "is true" of a given statement cannot change merely because we have increased our knowledge. But the fact is that we do use "is true" as though we are correct to affirm as true the statements which we currently count as true. We use "is true" as though we are *correct* to apply the truth predicate to the statements we currently hold true, even though we know that it is in principle possible that what we hold true today may not be held true in the future, just as we have revised statements which were previously held true. And, as I shall argue in part III, an implication of the fact that we treat our criteria *both* as determining the conditions under which it is correct for us to predicate "is true" of our statements *and* as being in principle revisable is that we need to revise our traditional picture of truth. We should not, therefore, accept an account of truth which respects the realist's intuition of truth in terms of correspondence with facts which could transcend our knowledge. And we should not join the antirealists in jettisoning the notion of truth out of respect for this intuition. For the conception of truth conditions in terms of criteria provides us with a way of arguing against the very idea of transcendent truth.

## 3. Antirealism Revisited

Wittgenstein's view that criteria determine truth conditions undercuts the realist thought motivating semantic antirealism, namely, that some sentences might have truth conditions which transcend our ability to recognize them. For, as we have seen, Wittgenstein's novel conception of a truth condition links the truth condition of every sentence in language which is treated as being true or false with the way that the sentence is used. Wittgenstein held that in every area of discourse or, in his terminology, in every type of language game, we predicate "is true" of a sentence because the satisfaction of the criterion governing it decisively establishes it as true. For by linguistic convention, if the criterion of a claim is met, it is certain that a criterially governed claim is true. He further held that statements belonging to different language games, for example, "It is true that Jones is in pain," "It is true that C.M. was born in 1961," and "It is true that Moses lived" are used differently in the context of affirming and denying them although we predicate "is true" of each of them. Because they belong to different language games, we recognize different kinds of criteria as decisive for establishing their truth. The criterion that Jones is in pain is Jones's pain behavior coupled with a criterion that he is not merely pretending. And the criterion that C.M. was born in 1961 is one type of record, while the criterion that Moses lived is yet another type of record which would be considered insufficient to establish the truth of a statement of the former type. Therefore, while it is possible to be certain of each of these types of statements, they are different kinds of certain propositions; that is, they are used to express different kinds of certainty. As Wittgenstein describes the difference between different types of statements which we treat as being true or false in our language,

I can be as certain of someone else's sensations as of any fact. But this does not make the propositions, "He is much depressed," "25 × 25 = 625," and "I am sixty years old" into similar instruments. The explanation suggests itself that the certainty is of a different kind. This seems to point to a psychological process. But the difference is logical. . . . The kind of certainty is the kind of language game. (*P.I.*, p. 224)

Wittgenstein cautions us not to infer from the fact that we accept different kinds of statements as true upon different kinds of grounds that some statements to which we apply the predicate "is true" are more certain than others or that the predicate "is true" is actually misapplied to some sentences. For example, we should not think that because the certainty expressed by the statement "It is true that he is depressed" is different from the certainty expressed by "It is true that I am sixty" and "It is true that 25 × 25 = 625," the first statement involves a misuse of the predicate "is true" because we can never definitively determine whether it is true. For every statement in language which we treat as being true or false is treated as being true or false because we have a criterion of its truth which counts as an adequate test of a statement within that language game. That is to say, we call a proposition true or false when we have a conventional way of determining whether it is true which we intersubjectively agree upon as being decisive for establishing the truth of that type of statement. And naturally, what counts as an adequate test of one type of statement is different from what counts as an adequate test of another type. This does not mean that statements such as "He is in pain" in contrast to statements such as "She lives on Charles Street West" are not determinately true or false or do not have truth conditions. Rather, it means that the former type of statement is not used to express the same kind of certainty as the latter, for we employ different kinds of criteria in determining the truth of each.

Antirealists assume that because we cannot ascertain the truth values of statements referring to the remote past or to other peoples' mental states in the same way that we can ascertain the truth values of other types of statements, the former are not determinately true or false, and our conventional practice of treating them as bivalent is inaccurate. Wittgenstein's answer to this is that we should not expect to be able to ascertain the truth values of each type of truth functional statement in the same way before we are prepared to predicate "is true" of each of them. We should keep in mind that what we treat as an adequate test of one statement is different from what we treat as being an adequate test of another. As Wittgenstein remarks,

"What is internal is hidden from us."—The future is hidden from us. But does an astronomer think like this when he calculates an eclipse of the sun? If I see someone writhing in pain with evident cause, I do not think: all the same, his feelings are hidden from me. (*P.I.*, p. 223)

We cannot find out whether future-tense statements are true in the same way that we can determine the truth of statements about the present. But given that statements about the future are used to make predictions, we are as entitled to call them true on the basis on which we make them as we are in classifying statements about the present as true on the grounds upon which we assert these.

Antirealists who claim that we are incorrect in classifying some statements as bivalent depart from Wittgenstein in that they refuse to take the way in which we use a statement as relevant to whether we should treat it as determinately true or false. But Wittgenstein would claim that if truth is to be an explicable concept, then the way in which we use a statement must be taken as being relevant to whether we can classify it as bivalent. And what it means to call a statement true varies across different language games as our manner of calculating truth values varies in different areas of discourse. Thus, once we realize the nuances in our uses of the predicate "is true," the idea that statements about the past are not determinately true or false because we cannot verify them in the same way that we can verify statements about the recent past reflects a failure to see the significance of the fact that "Moses lived" and "C.M. was born in 1961" are not used to make the same type of assertion.[1]

According to Wittgenstein, the only way for a statement to have a truth condition transcending our capacity for knowledge would be for a statement to be governed by a criterion which we could never ascertain as having been met. But this is not a logical possibility. It is possible that in a particular case it might be a contingent fact that we might be unable to ascertain whether the criterion of a claim was met. In John Canfield's example, we might make the criterion of a chess player's being a grandmaster his having a particular rating. And it is possible that in a particular case, the records of a chess player's rating might be destroyed so that we might be contingently unable to determine whether the criterion of his being a grandmaster had been met.[2] But in Wittgenstein's view, it is not logically possible for a statement which we treat as being true or false to be governed by a criterion which we could never, *in principle*, recognize as having been met. For he connects meaning with use, and knowing the circumstances under which to predicate "is true" of a sentence which we treat as being true or false is part of knowing how to use that sentence. Therefore, such a sentence could not be governed by a criterion which we could never, in principle, recognize as having been met, for in that case we could never have learned when to predicate "is true" of a sentence which we treat as having a truth value. That is, a sentence which we treat as being true or false could not logically be governed by a criterion which we could never recognize as having been met, for in that case, we could never have learned how to use the sentence.

To be sure, we can think of declarative sentences which lack criteria of truth. One such sentence is the inverted spectrum hypothesis which Wittgenstein mentions at *P.I.* #272, that one section of mankind might have one sensation of red and another section another.[3] But precisely because this type of sentence has no criterion of truth, we cannot, contrary to first impressions, treat it as being true or false. And therefore, Wittgenstein argues, we cannot properly classify it as a hypothesis or a proposition or as any other type of sentence which we think of as bearing a truth value. What Wittgenstein says about the inverted spectrum hypothesis at *P.I.* #272 is not that it is possible to make it although it is unverifiable. Rather, he says that on the assumption that the word "red" refers to a private exemplar, the hypothesis *would* be possible, though unverifiable. But this consequence shows the absurdity of that assumption. For if the meaning of the word "red" were taken as something that each person could know only from his own case rather than as the concept which we acquire when we learn what we are to *call* "red,"[4] then it is not clear what it could mean to question or affirm that something was red. For in that case, there could be no normative standard of what counts as being red. Consequently, the word "red" could not have any intersubjective meaning; we could never have learned to use it in sentences ascribing the quality of being red to objects. Given that the word "red" does have an intersubjective meaning, it is absurd to suppose that we could construe its meaning as its private reference rather than as its use.

By parity of reasoning, it is absurd to think of the inverted spectrum hypothesis, which rests on the assumption of private reference, as a possible hypothesis or proposition or as the sort of thing which we really think of as being either true or false. For we could only have come to think of it as a true or false proposition if we treated it as being true or false in our language, that is, if we used it in the contexts of affirming it and denying it. Or, as Wittgenstein puts it, we could only have come to think of it as a proposition if, *in our language*, we applied the calculus of truth functions to it. But we cannot apply the calculus of truth functions to the inverted spectrum hypothesis, that is, we cannot use it in the contexts of affirming it and denying it, because there is no criterion whereby we could predicate "is true" or "is false" of it. And this means that we can never have learned the circumstances under which we should affirm it as true. Hence, Wittgenstein's view is that every sentence which is treated as being true or false in our language is treated as being true or false only insofar as we have a criterion whereby we predicate "is true" of it, which tells us the grounds on which to affirm a statement of that type. For it is by learning the grounds or criterion of a sentence that we learn how to use such a sentence in the context of making affirmations and denials. Thus, Wittgenstein's conception of the truth condition of a sentence in terms of the use of the sentence undermines the realist thought that some sentences may have truth conditions transcending our ability to recognize them.

# PART II

# From "Meaning is Use" to Semantic Antirealism

We have seen how Wittgenstein's conception of meaning as use leads to his rejection of transcendent truth: if we conceive of the truth condition of a sentence in terms of the way in which we use the sentence, then a sentence could not have a truth condition which we could not recognize as obtaining. If it had a transcendent truth condition, we would not have come to treat it as being true or false. Michael Dummett reads the dictum that meaning is use as implying the rejection of a truth-conditional account of meaning. He claims that it has inspired a position which he terms "semantic antirealism," namely that we do not come to understand our sentences by learning what it is that would make them true. For Dummett thinks that rejecting transcendent truth entails rejecting truth *tout court*. According to Dummett, the crux of the dictum that meaning is use is that what a speaker's understanding consists in must be manifestable in his use of language. And he holds that there are some sentences which we treat as being determinately true or false, or bivalent, for which we are not in a position to determine their truth values. Therefore, since there is no practical ability through which we could manifest our knowledge of these sentences' truth conditions, we must reject the thought that we understand these sentences by learning to recognize their truth conditions as obtaining when they obtain. Thus, we must also reject the notion that the general form of explanation of meaning is that the meaning of a statement is its truth conditions. We must hold instead that, in the case of undecidable sentences, we grasp their meanings by learning to recognize conditions under which we are justified in asserting them where these fall short of being decisive for establishing their truth.[1]

I will argue that Dummett's attempt to read semantic antirealism into Wittgenstein is out of the spirit of "meaning is use" as Wittgenstein intended the dictum. First of all, I will show that Dummett's notion that certain sentences which we treat as bivalent in fact have no truth values rests upon a realist conception of truth. That is, Dummett's argument rests upon the assumption that the only possible way to construe what it is to determine a sentence's truth value is in terms of recognizing the obtaining of a realist truth condition. And, thus, his argument ultimately rests on a refusal to recognize an alternative account of what it is to determine the truth value of a sentence which falls out of the dictum that meaning is use: namely, that to determine the truth value of a sentence is to learn to apply a conventional rule which tells us the grounds upon which we may predicate "is true" of the sentence. I will further argue that the premises Dummett requires to draw his antirealist conclusion are in tension with an account of meaning as use. Specifically, we shall see that Dummett's argument for rejecting a truth-conditional account of meaning depends on a commitment to molecularism. Yet, as I shall argue, the notion that meaning is use entails a holistic view of meaning. That is, it implies that a sentence has meaning only in the context of an entire language. And once we accept the holism implicit in an account of meaning as use, Dummett's argument for semantic antirealism does not go through.

Another of my aims here is to show that semantic antirealism in itself is not a coherent position. There is a tension between Dummett's verificationism and his commitment to truth as correspondence: He is led to reject the possibility of a truth-conditional account of meaning because he is torn between his desire to hold, with the realist, that if something is true there must be something in the world in virtue of which it is true and his desire to say, with Wittgenstein, that if something is true we must be able to know that it is. But if we do accept that the concept "truth" is internally related to our capacity for knowledge, then the fact that a sentence corresponds to no perceptible segment of reality is irrelevant to the question of whether it is true or false. Wittgenstein's account of truth is to be preferred to antirealism partly because the former is consistent with the initial motivation for rejecting realism. For if we hold that the realist cannot give content to his conception of truth on the grounds that it outruns our use, then we can only hold that truth conditions are determined by criteria. Thus, Wittgenstein's more radical break with the realist/correspondence tradition is grounded in a deeper commitment to the thought that meaning is use.

## 4. The Acquisition Argument
## and the Manifestation Criterion

Dummett's project in his "What Is a Theory of Meaning"[1] articles is to argue that a theory of meaning based on truth conditions cannot give content to what a speaker's knowledge consists in. He argues that when we learn a language, we do not, in general, come to understand our sentences by learning what it is that would render them true. Thus, the general form of an explanation of meaning is not a statement of a sentence's truth conditions. Dummett claims to base this position, which he terms "semantic antirealism," on Wittgenstein's notion that meaning is use. His defense of this position rests on the following line of argument: (1) that a speaker's understanding must be manifestable and (2) that what counts as manifestation of a speaker's understanding of some concept cannot outrun the way this understanding was initially acquired. He presents this case as follows.

He first points out that we expect a theory of meaning to give an account of how language users communicate by means of it or of "what makes language function as language" ("What Is a Theory of Meaning I," henceforth "WTM I," p. 99). That is, a theory of meaning ought to make explicit the principles regulating our use of language which we already implicitly grasp. According to Dummett, if we are to grant Wittgenstein's thought that "to grasp the meaning of an expression is to understand its role in the language" ("WTM I," p. 99), then the problem for a theory of meaning is to describe the knowledge that a speaker has when he knows the meaning of an expression, which has to be in terms of some capacity to use it. A theory of meaning ought to articulate the ability that speakers of a language have and analyze it into distinct components. It should do so first by *representing* linguistic ability as a set of propositions which a speaker would have to know in order to understand a language, including axioms specifying the reference of terms and the applications of predicates. And, second, it should specify some practical ability for each of these propositions by which a speaker could demonstrate his knowledge of it. That is, if part of understanding a sentence is knowing how to use it, then if a theory of meaning is to say what a speaker's understanding of a given sentence consists in, it must specify some observable linguistic skill which this understanding is to issue in. The lesson we should learn from "meaning is use" is that "a theory of meaning is required to make the workings of language open to view. To know a language is to be able to employ a language" ("WTM I," p. 100). Hence,

> Where we are concerned with a theoretical representation of understanding in terms of propositional knowledge of some practical ability, and, in particular, where that practical ability is precisely the mastery of language, it is incumbent on us, if our theory of meaning is to be explanatory... to specify not only what someone has to know for him to have that ability, but also what it is for him to have that knowledge, that is, what we are taking as constituting a manifestation of knowledge of those propositions; if we fail to do this, the connection will not be made between the theoretical representation and the practical ability it is supposed to represent. ("WTM I," p. 121)

Meaning is not a private matter, for language is essentially communicable; to understand a sentence is to know how to use it. Thus, if a theory of meaning is to give content to what a speaker's understanding consists in, it must describe how that understanding is to be manifested. For each sentence that a speaker is said to grasp, the theory must specify some practical ability, the possession of which constitutes knowledge of the meaning of that sentence.

Dummett makes the further point that in order for a theory of meaning to give content to what a speaker's knowledge consists in, it must specify how a speaker could master his own mother tongue. That is, it cannot merely explain how a foreigner, who has already acquired the concepts expressible in his own language, could learn how to interpret another language. Rather, it must say how a native speaker initially acquires the concepts he learns when he learns to speak his own language. Thus, Dummett holds that a theory of meaning can only explain what language mastery consists in if it is molecular, that is, if it assumes that an agent attains mastery of a language one piece at a time. A holistic theory of meaning, which holds that a fragment of language makes sense only within the context of an entire language, cannot explain what language mastery consists in. For holism provides no way of segmenting the ability to use language as a whole into distinct component abilities ("WTM I," p. 116). And thus it cannot provide an account of how language acquisition takes place. As Dummett puts this point,

> The difference between a molecular and a holistic view of language is... that on a holistic view, it is impossible fully to understand any sentence without knowing the entire language,

whereas, on a molecular view, there is, for each sentence, a determinate fragment of language knowledge of which suffices for a complete understanding of that sentence. Such a conception . . . seems to be required if we are to allow for the progressive acquisition of a language. On a holistic view, on the other hand, there can be nothing between not knowing the language at all and knowing it completely. ("WTM II," p. 79)

Thus, according to Dummett, only a theory of meaning which is molecular rather than holistic can give an account of how an agent acquires mastery of a language and, hence, of what the ability to speak a language consists in. For molecularism "allows for the arrangement of expressions and sentences in a language according as the understanding of an expression is or is not dependent on the prior understanding of another" ("WTM II," p. 79). And it holds that there is a ground level of sentences which we initially acquire, knowledge of which presupposes no prior knowledge of a language.

Dummett identifies what a speaker's understanding consists in with what he terms his "implicit knowledge." That is, he identifies it with the knowledge of the meaning of those sentences which we can learn without having any prior linguistic competence—in other words, with the sentences containing the most basic elements of language, such as the references of terms and the applications of predicates. For according to Dummett, it is these sentences which represent what mastery of one's mother tongue consists in; if a foreigner who did not know the language were to memorize them, then assuming that he could make fast enough inferences, his linguistic behavior would match that of the native speaker.[2] Because these sentences can be grasped by someone who has no prior knowledge of a language, Dummett holds that a speaker's understanding of them must be manifested nonverbally. Such understanding cannot be manifested by an ability to express a sentence by means of an equivalent sentence. For, according to Dummett, if we want to discover what a speaker's understanding of his native tongue consists in, we must examine the way in which it was initially acquired. And what counts as manifestation of this knowledge cannot outrun the way it was initially acquired. He argues that

it would be self-defeating to require that [a] speaker's knowledge of the propositions constituting the theory of meaning for the language should be manifested in an ability to formulate them verbally since the fundamental aim of the theoretical representation is to explain what someone who does not yet

know any language has to acquire in order to come to know
the given language. ("WTM II," p. 70)

Dummett thinks that we cannot allow what counts as manifestation of a speaker's understanding to be a capacity to give verbal explanations. Such a capacity presupposes that a speaker already has
considerable linguistic ability, and so it does not distinguish what a
child must learn in order to master his own language from what a
foreigner must know in order to interpret another language. And what
we want from a theory of meaning is that it should explain the initial
acquisition of our concepts. Thus, if, for example, we want to say that
in mastering a language, we come to understand our sentences by
learning what it is for them to be true, we must give an account of what
it is to know this which does not presuppose prior knowledge of the
sentence. To ask what our concept of truth consists in is to ask where
our implicit grasp of the concept comes in, that is, how the concept is
initially acquired. Therefore, manifestation of a speaker's grasp of what
it is for a sentence to be true cannot in general consist in his capacity
to verbally state the truth condition or we will never get a handle on
how the concept was initially acquired. As Dummett puts this point,

> An ability to state the truth condition of a sentence is no more
> than an ability to express the content of the sentence in other
> words. We accept such capacity as evidence of a grasp of the
> meaning of the original sentence on the presumption that the
> speaker understands the words in which he is stating the truth
> condition, but at some point it must be possible to break out
> of the circle. (*Truth and Other Enigmas,* henceforth *T.O.E.* [Cam-
> bridge, Mass.: Harvard University Press, 1978], p. 224)

In other words, knowledge of meaning can be either implicit or explicit. It is explicit when a speaker can state what he knows, that is,
when he can assert some sentences that express the content of his
knowledge (and then, of course, it is implied that he knows the meaning of the sentences he asserts). But it would be circular (and thus, as
Dummett says, "self-defeating") to explain all knowledge of meaning as
explicit knowledge, for any such explanation presupposes what it is to
know the meaning of some sentences. Hence, knowledge of meaning
must in the end be explained in terms of implicit knowledge, that is,
in terms of some practical ability.[3] And, therefore, if we want an account of what a speaker's understanding of a truth condition amounts
to, then what counts as manifestation of this knowledge may not be his

ability to state what it is. Instead, it must issue in his ability to recognize the truth condition of a sentence as obtaining when it obtains.

Armed with the principle that manifestation of a speaker's knowledge must issue in a recognitional capacity, Dummett proceeds to argue that we must reject a truth-conditional theory of meaning. That is, he denies that our understanding of our language can be explained in terms of our learning, for each sentence, what it is for it to be true. For, according to Dummett, natural language is full of sentences with truth conditions which we could not recognize as obtaining. That is, we treat many sentences as being determinately true or false which are not effectively decidable, that is, for which "we have no effective procedure which will, in a finite amount of time, put us into a position in which we can recognize whether the truth condition of a statement is satisfied" (*T.O.E.*, p. 16). Examples of such sentences include subjunctive conditionals and those which refer to regions of space-time in principle inaccessible to us such as the remote past or future. With undecidable sentences, we cannot give content to ascribing implicit knowledge of what the truth condition is to a speaker since there is no practical ability by which this knowledge could be manifested. And, thus, we cannot hold that we learn the meanings of these sentences by learning to recognize their truth conditions. Therefore, we cannot adopt a theory of meaning which assumes that bivalence must hold across the board. That is, we cannot maintain that, in general, we come to understand our sentences by learning to recognize their truth conditions. For many sentences in language are such that we can give no account of how we acquire the concept of what it is for them to be true.

According to Dummett, we assume we have a grasp of what it is for our sentences to be true because we employ a two-valued logic. We treat certain inference forms as valid, which presuppose that bivalence holds across our sentences. And, thus, we think we have a grasp of what their truth value consists in. In fact, however, we learn the inference forms of classical logic only after we have mastered our language. Therefore, our bivalent logical practice does not explain our acquisition of the concept of truth. It merely explains our belief that we have the concept. As Dummett argues, classical logic depends for its justification on our having the notions of truth and falsity which license the assumption of bivalence. Thus, a mere training in a practice cannot itself generate the notion of truth unless we already have it ("WTM II," p. 102).

It might be objected that if semantic antirealism is supposed to be inspired by the dictum that meaning is use, then a community's treatment of a statement as determinately true or false should suffice for us to attribute to its members a grasp of the truth condition. We might argue that a speaker manifests his grasp of what the truth value of a statement consists in merely through his bivalent logical practice. Such an account of what counts as manifestation would appear to be consistent with the thought that meaning is use: if a word has meaning in virtue of its intersubjective use within a community, then a sentence has whatever meaning a community's use confers on it. All that is required for a community member to grasp a concept expressible in his language is that he be trained in a linguistic practice.

Dummett rejects the thought that our existing practice suffices to explain our grasp of the concept of truth. He holds that we cannot assume at the outset that our bivalent logical practice does not stand in need of revision. According to Dummett, the task of a semantic theory is to tell us what model we must have for the meanings of our sentences if our inferences are justified (*T.O.E.*, p. 311). Thus, what we seek is not merely a description of our practice. We want a theory of meaning that is capable of criticizing it. In order to provide such a potentially revisionist theory of meaning, we must assume at the outset that meaning holism is false. We cannot allow the unit of meaning to be no smaller than the entire language. For if we want a theory of meaning to be capable of criticizing a practice, we must have a way of distinguishing good inferences from bad ones. And since inferences are valid partly in virtue of meaning, such a criticism would have to be leveled at the meanings of the sentences. But if we are holists, we will be unable to make this kind of criticism. For if we assume that a sentence has meaning only in the context of a language, then a sentence will have meaning just in virtue of its use. That is, it will have whatever meaning our use has already given it. Therefore, if we want a semantic theory to show us where we must revise a practice, a sentence must be taken as saying something on its own. That is, there must be, for each sentence, "a representation of its content which is independent of the description of the entire language to which the sentence belongs" (*T.O.E.*, p. 304). As Dummett argues,

> [t]he possibility that a language may stand in need of adjustment... is implicit in the idea that a language ought to be capable of systematization by... a molecular theory of meaning for there [is] no guarantee that a complex of linguistic practices which has grown up by piecemeal historical evolution... will conform to any systematic theory. ("WTM II," p. 104)

> [t]he idea, which Wittgenstein held, that acceptance of any principle of inference contributes to determining the mean-

ings of the words involved, and therefore, since speakers of a language may confer on their words whatever meanings they choose, forms of inference generally accepted are unassailable by philosophical criticism has its home only within a holistic view of language. If language ought to be capable of systematization by a molecular theory of meaning, we are not free to choose any logic we like, but only one for which it is possible to provide a semantics which accords with the other uses to which our sentences are put; in accepting or rejecting any... form of inference, we are responsible to the meanings of the logical constants, thought of as given in some uniform manner (e.g., by two- or many-valued truth tables). ("WTM II," p. 105)

On a molecular view of meaning, our acceptance of an inference presupposing the bivalence of a statement does not justify attributing to us a grasp of what its truth value consists in. We may believe that a statement is determinately true or false only because we employ a two-valued logic system. But classical logic may be incorrect; it may license invalid inferences. In Dummett's example, we cannot infer from a community's acceptance as a valid principle of inference the alternation of opposing counterfactuals that counterfactuals *are* bivalent. For if a speaker cannot explain how to verify a counterfactual (such as "Jones would have proven brave had his courage ever been tested"), then he cannot give content to what its truth value must consist in. Hence, wherever there are sentences for which we cannot say what our implicit grasp of their truth conditions consists in, we must revise our practice of treating them as bivalent. We must abandon descriptivism in favor of revisionism, for we can no longer hold that we learn the meanings of these sentences by learning to recognize their truth conditions. We must hold instead that we learn to recognize the situations in which we are justified in asserting them.

Dummett concedes that rejecting a truth-conditional account of the meanings of certain sentences will lead to counterintuitive results. For example, in denying that statements about the past are determinately true or false, the antirealist will be denying the truth value link between statements referring to the remote past and present-tense statements made in the remote past. We are all inclined to say that what makes a past-tense statement, made in the present, true is the fact that the same statement, made long ago in the present tense, *was* true. The antirealist denies that it is from an understanding of the truth value link that we grasp what it is for a past-tense statement to be true. As he argues, we learn the use of the past tense by learning to recognize certain situations as justifying statements expressed in that tense. And there is no way we could pass from a grasp of the kind of situation which justifies asserting a past-tense statement to a grasp of what it would be for such a statement to be true independently of any situation which would justify us in asserting it *now*. In other words,

> the only notion of truth for past tense statements which we could have acquired through our training in their use is one which coincides with the justifiability of assertions of such statements, i.e., with the existence of situations which we are capable of recognizing as obtaining and which justify such as-sertions. We are not therefore entitled to say, of any arbitrary statement about the past, that it must be true or false indepen-dently of our present or future knowledge, or capacity for knowledge, of its truth value. (*T.O.E.*, p. 363)

Thus, the antirealist account of statements about the past is incompatible with acknowledging a truth value link between differently tensed state-ments uttered at different times, for if it follows from the truth of some present-tense statement S that a past-tense statement S', uttered in the future will be true, then it follows that S' will not just be true in virtue of something we could recognize as justifying us in asserting it. It might still be true even if we had no evidence of it. The antirealist rejects this thought by relating the truth value of past-tense statements not to the evidence that was available for them at the time of evaluation referred to but to the evidence that is available *now*. Dummett admits that the notion of a truth value link appears to be a fundamental part of our understand-ing of past-tense statements: he admits that he, like everyone else, feels a strong undertow toward realism here. But he holds that this is one of those "errors of thought to which the human mind seems naturally prone" and, as such, it is one of those cases where we must be revisionists about language. Since we could not grasp the truth conditions of statements about the remote past through our training in their use, we must bite the bullet and say that the only account we can give of their meaning is in terms of the conditions which justify asserting them.

## 5. Antirealism Presupposes Realism

What are we to make of Dummett's argument for rejecting a truth conditional account of meaning? First of all, it should be noted that it presupposes a commitment to a realist conception of truth which the later Wittgenstein explicitly rejected. That is to say, Dummett's belief that some statements which we treat as being determinately true or false have truth conditions which we could never recognize as obtaining rests upon a realist conception of truth conditions. That is, it rests upon an assumption that the only thing that could make a given statement true is its correspondence with some segment of reality in virtue of which it is true. For Dummett assumes that our assumption of bivalence for a given statement can only be explained by ascribing to us a belief that *something in the world* must make such a statement true. And it is only because he makes this initial assumption that Dummett is led to hold that certain statements are problematic for a truth-conditional theory of meaning, given his thought that if something is true it must be possible for us to determine its truth value. In other words, it is only because Dummett assumes that the claim "p is true" amounts to the claim that there is something in virtue of which it is true that he is led to his antirealist conclusion, namely, that we treat certain statements as being true or false for which we can give no content to what our grasp of their truth conditions consists in. This becomes clear when we examine Dummett's argument that unless we revise our linguistic practice, we will be imputing to ourselves a grasp of the notion of truth that goes beyond any knowledge which we could manifest in our use. Dummett writes,

> the correspondence theory expresses one important feature of the concept of truth. . . : that a statement is true only if there is something in the world *in virtue of which* it is true. . . . Realism consists in the belief that for *any* statement there is something in virtue of which either it or its negation is true: it is only on the basis of this belief that we can justify the idea that truth and falsity play an essential role in the notion of the meaning of a statement, that the general form of explanation of meaning is a statement of the truth-conditions. (*T.O.E.*, p. 14, second emphasis mine)

What Dummett is alluding to here is a tension between what he sees as the two central features of the concept of truth: on the one hand, he holds that it is part of the concept of truth that if something is true, there must be some segment of reality in virtue of which it is true (what he calls "Principle C" in "What is a Theory of Meaning II"). And, on the other hand, he holds that if something is true, it must be possible for us to know that it is true (which he terms "Principle K"). Dummett believes that certain statements—that is, subjunctive conditionals and those which refer to the remote past and future—are problematic for the view that the general form of an explanation of meaning is a statement of the truth conditions. For since we cannot point to any tangible segment of reality in virtue of which such statements are true, there seems to be no way that we could tell whether they are true. And, given Principle K, it then seems that we cannot give content to saying that they have truth conditions. Dummett argues that the only way we can justify our assumption of bivalence for these problematic statements is by adopting a realist account of what their truth value consists in—that is, by assuming that there *is* some segment of reality in virtue of which they are true, even though that reality is inaccessible to us. For example, Dummett holds that we assume bivalence for statements about the remote past because

> we are inclined to think of statements in the past tense as being rendered true or false by a reality which is no longer accessible to us . . . but which nevertheless is in some sense still there, for if there were, as it were, nothing left of the past, then there would be nothing to make a true statement about the past true, nothing in virtue of which it would be true. On such a picture . . . our knowledge of what actually makes such statements true or false involves our understanding of what it would be to apprehend their truth directly, i.e., by that which actually rendered them true. To be able to do this would be to be capable of observing the past as we do the present, that is, to be able to survey the whole of reality . . . from a position outside the time-sequence. . . . We cannot do this; but we know just what powers a superhuman observer would have to have in order to be able to do it—a hypothetical being for whom the sentences in question would *not* be undecidable. And we tacitly suppose that it is in our conception of the powers which this superhuman observer would have to have, and how he would determine the truth values of the sentences, that our understanding of their truth conditions consists. ("W.T.M. II," p. 98)

Dummett holds that the only account we can give of our grasp of the truth conditions of what he calls "undecidable statements" must involve imputing to us powers of observation which we do not possess. For statements about the remote past, Dummett holds that we imagine what a superhuman being might observe who could survey the past from a perspective outside of the time sequence. For counterfactual statements such as "Jones would have proven brave, had his courage ever been tested," Dummett says that we imagine some extraordinary type of fact, perhaps known only to God, in virtue of which it is true. For example, we might imagine that courage consists in a spiritual mechanism rather than in its behavioral manifestations so that "Jones is brave" would have been already true or false before his courage was *revealed* by his encountering danger. (*T.O.E.*, p. 15)

However, Dummett holds that this type of account will not suffice to explain our grasp of the truth conditions of undecidable statements. For it plainly does not describe the way we actually do determine the truth values of these statements. And thus, it does not explain how we learn to use them in the context of predicating "is true" and "is false" of them. That is, it does not explain how we come to treat them as being bivalent. As Dummett remarks,

> Anyone with a sufficient degree of sophistication will reject [the] belief in a spiritual mechanism. . . . His ground for rejecting the argument is that if such a statement as "Jones was brave" is true, it must be true in virtue of the sort of fact which we have been taught to regard as justifying us in asserting it. It cannot be true in virtue of some quite different sort of fact of which we can have no direct knowledge, for otherwise the statement "Jones was brave" would not have the meaning that *we* have given it. (*T.O.E.*, p. 16)

Dummett argues that since we cannot give content to our grasp of the truth conditions of these undecidable sentences in a way which is consistent with our actual use of them, we must give up the thought that an explanation of their meaning can be given in terms of their truth conditions. We must accept that for this type of statement, we can no longer explain their meaning by laying down the truth conditions, but by stipulating the conditions under which they may be asserted. The justification for this change is that this is how we in fact learn to use these statements (*T.O.E.*, p. 18). In other words, we ought not to treat undecidable statements as being determinately true or false for,

> We are entitled to say that a statement p must be either true or false, that there must be something in virtue of which it either is true or is false, only when p is a statement of such a kind that we could in a finite amount of time bring ourselves into a position in which we were justified either in asserting or denying p. . . . The notions of truth and falsehood cannot be satisfactorily explained once we leave the realm of effectively decidable statements. (*T.O.E.*, p. 16–18)

Thus, Dummett holds that we cannot adopt a theory of meaning which assumes that bivalence holds, across the board, for any class of sentences without attributing to ourselves a grasp of the notion of truth which goes beyond any knowledge which we could manifest in our actual use of language. As he puts this point,

> There is . . . no possible alternative account of that in which our grasp of the truth conditions of such statements consists: but this one works only by imputing to us an apprehension of the way in which those sentences might be used by beings very unlike ourselves, and, in doing so, fails to answer the question how we come to be able to assign our sentences a meaning which is dependent on a use to which we are unable to put them. . . . There is no way of distinguishing such an account from the thesis that we treat certain of our sentences as if their use resembled that of other sentences in certain respects in which it in fact does not; that is, that we systematically misunderstand our own language. ("WTM II," pp. 100–101)

Thus, the argument for semantic antirealism can be summed up as follows: If we assume that bivalence holds for every class of sentences which we *treat* as being determinately true or false, we will be imputing to ourselves a grasp of truth conditions which we could never recognize as obtaining. Therefore, we cannot maintain that the *general* form of an explanation of meaning is a statement of a sentence's truth conditions, for this would mean attributing to ourselves a grasp of the concept of truth which we could not manifest in our use.[1]

Dummett's argument for rejecting a truth-conditional theory of meaning presupposes that a realist conception of truth conditions is the only one that is available to us. His conclusion that the notions of truth and falsity cannot be satisfactorily explained for undecidable statements such as those about the remote past only seems plausible if we believe that what makes a true statement true is its correspondence with some fact or some segment of reality in virtue of which it is true. It is only if we conceive of a truth condition in this realist manner, that is, in terms of correspondence between a statement and a fact, that it seems as though the only thing that could make a past-tense statement true would be its correspondence to a now no-longer-existent segment of reality. And it is only if we conceive of the truth condition of a past-tense statement in this way that we will hold that determining its truth value must involve surveying the past as we do the present. Thus, it is only on a realist conception of truth conditions that it is obviously impossible for us to determine the truth value of statements about the remote past. And, a fortiori, it is only on a realist conception of truth that there is a problem explaining what our understanding of the truth condition of a past-tense statement consists in for someone who is committed to the verificationist thought expressed by Principle K.

However, we need not accept the realist's conception of truth. Nor need we think of the truth conditions of our sentences in terms of their correspondence to facts. I have argued that it is open to us to think of truth not in terms of correspondence but in terms of use. We can hold, as Wittgenstein does, that our use or treatment of a statement as being determinately true or false means that we have a conventional way of testing it which we accept as establishing it as either true or false. That is, we can hold that the truth conditions of our statements are determined by our conventional ways of finding out whether they are true or false, or by our conventional rules for predicating "is true" of them. Or, to put the point another way, we can hold that a truth condition is determined by a linguistic rule or convention which tells us the grounds upon which we may affirm the statement. If we do conceive of truth conditions in terms of criteria or conventions, we will be sensitive to the differences between the kinds of statements that we treat as true or false, and between the areas of discourse to which they belong. For to think of a truth condition in this way is to think of it as a rule which tells us how to use a given statement in certain contexts. And statements belonging to different language games are used differently in the context of predicating "is true" and "is false" of them: Our methods of testing them differ, the definitiveness of our tests may differ in different areas of discourse, and, consequently, what we mean by calling a statement true will depend on the type of statement it is and the type of language game to which it belongs. Thus, it follows that if we think of a truth condition as a linguistic rule governing our use of "It is true that p," we will bear in mind how we might go about testing the type of statement in question when we determine what our criterion or convention for applying the truth predicate to it must be.

If we conceive of the truth conditions of our sentences in terms of the way in which we use them, we will not be tempted by Dummett's thought that "the notions of truth and falsity cannot be satisfactorily explained once we leave the realm of effectively decidable sentences." This thought was originally inspired by mathematical conjectures for which we lack an effective decision procedure, such as Goldbach's Conjecture that every even number greater than two is the sum of two primes. The antirealist holds that it is natural to say that Goldbach's Conjecture must be determinately true or false even though we have not yet been able to prove or refute it.[2] And he holds that because we do not have a way of proving it, it constitutes an example of a mathematical proposition whose truth value transcends our recognitional capacities. But, as

Wittgenstein argues, this thought betrays a misunderstanding of the nature of mathematical conjectures. A mathematical conjecture has the character of a heuristic device which may someday lead to the construction of a proof. It does not have the character of a mathematical *proposition* which is *already* true or false although we do not yet know its truth value.[3] For a mathematical conjecture differs from a mathematical proposition in that there are no rules governing its use, for it is not yet part of a system of propositions for which we have a general method of verifying them. Consequently, a mathematical conjecture cannot be true or false, for the concept of mathematical truth only applies to expressions for which we understand how to determine their truth value. As Stuart Shanker argues, it is not that we cannot assert a proposition before we have constructed a proof for it; it is that we cannot understand a string of symbols until we have constructed a rule for its use. Or to put the point another way, it is not that the truth value of Goldbach's Conjecture transcends our recognitional capacities, but that no thought has been expressed by it at all[4] for "[w]here we have no logical method for finding a solution, the question doesn't make sense either" (*P.R.* #151). Hence, Goldbach's Conjecture is not an example of a case where our concept of truth cannot be explained. Rather, the situation is that we have *no* concept of its truth for we have no rule which would govern our use of it in the context of predicating "is true" and "is false" of it. By contrast, in the language games in which we do have rules for predicating "is true" of our sentences, we are not in general at a loss to determine the truth value of a statement which we *treat* as being true or false. For any ground we might have for establishing a given type of sentence as true appears an effective way of deciding its truth value once we consider what is *meant* by affirming a statement within that type of language game. That is, any method we have of testing one of the statements which we treat as being true or false appears an adequate way of deciding its truth value once we take into account the way that the statement is used. And, given the differences among the language games in which we predicate "is true" of our sentences, we will not expect each test of a statement to establish its truth value with the same degree of conclusiveness. As Wittgenstein puts this point,

> That the evidence makes someone else's feeling *merely* probable is not what matters to us; what we are looking at is the fact that *this* is taken as *evidence* for something important; that we base a judgment on *this* involved sort of evidence, and hence that *such* evidence has a special importance in our lives and is

made prominent by a concept. (The "inner" and the "outer," a *picture*.) (*Z.* #554)

If we hold that statements such as "Jones is in pain" are not determinately true or false in contrast to statements about the weather because, unlike the latter, pain is not directly observable, we will be missing the point of making third-person ascriptions of pain. We will be missing the fact that the "uncertainty" involved in ascriptions of pain relates not to the particular case, but to the method or rules of evidence within that language game, and that there is *not* an uncertainty in *each particular case* (*Z.* #555, #556). In other words, just as our concepts of the outer are based on what is directly observable, our concept of pain is based, *inter alia*, on pain behavior. When we make a judgment about someone else's feeling, we base our judgment on *this* sort of evidence against a background of what we know about their veracity. Thus, given that we *do* treat statements such as "Jones is in pain" as being true or false, the question to ask is "What do we mean by affirming that 'he is in pain'?" In other words, how do we use this type of sentence? Plainly, when we say "It's true that Jones is in pain," we mean to assert that we have observed his pain behavior and that the question of doubt has not arisen. And we are understood to be using the statement in *this* way, rather than as we would use a statement such as "It really is snowing outside!" The fact that we are sometimes mistaken in our judgments about others' sensations and that the evidence makes our judgments merely probable is not what matters to us. The fact that the language game of ascriptions of pain admits of a different type of certainty than statements about the 'outer' does not mean that statements about others' sensations are not determinately true or false. What matters is the way we use the type of statement in question, and what we mean by predicating "is true" of it.[5]

A similar argument can be made against the view that statements about the remote past are not determinately true or false in contrast to statements about the present. For just as ascriptions of pain belong to a different language game from statements about the external world, our use of statements about the remote past is importantly different from our use of statements about the present. When we affirm the existence of a living figure such as Ronald Reagan, there are a multitude of attributes associated with the individual which we are definitely prepared to affirm of him, such as "was an actor," "is married to Nancy Reagan," "is Patty Davis's father," and other bits of information which are in public records. But when we affirm the existence of a figure such as Moses or William Tell, there are attributes associated with them which we are not prepared definitively to affirm or to deny (cf. *P.I.* #79). That is, there are things which are commonly said about Moses and William Tell which were once known to be true or false, but have now become part of legends surrounding persons who lived in the remote past. Thus, when we say, "It's true that William Tell lived," we mean something like, "There was a person called William Tell who lived in Austria under the Hapsburg Empire and who *may* have shot an apple off his son's head." That is, it may not be as clear just how much is involved in affirming a statement about the remote past as it is with respect to statements about the present. Yet we still treat statements such as "Moses lived" as being true or false. That is to say, statements about the remote past do not express the same type of certainty as statements about the present. But this is irrelevant to whether the former are true or false. The issue is what we mean by predicating "is true" of a statement about the remote past and what we are understood as saying.[6]

On an account of truth conditions in terms of criteria and conventions, we are no longer faced with Dummett's problem of "explaining how we come to be able to assign a meaning to our sentences which is dependent on a use to which we are unable to give them." For this dilemma presupposes that the use to which we *do* put our sentences is the sort of use to which a realist would put them. It only arises on the assumption that when we say "It's true that p," we mean "p corresponds to some segment of reality." But if we think of the truth conditions of our sentences in terms of their use, that is, if we hold that the meaning of "true" depends on the context in which it is uttered, it no longer makes sense to speak of "a use of our sentences to which we are unable to put them." For a truth condition is determined by a rule which tells us when we are to predicate "is true" of one of the sentences which we treat as being true or false. It is determined by a rule which tells us how we are to use a sentence in the context of judging its truth value. And a sentence could not be governed by a sort of rule for determining its truth value which it would be impossible for us to apply, for in that case, we would never have come to use that sentence in the context of affirming and denying it. Or, to put the point another way, a sentence which we treat as being true or false could not be governed by a criterion which we could never, in principle, recognize as having been met, for in that case we should never have come to treat the sentence as being true or false.

Dummett's argument that we must either give up our assumption of bivalence for certain statements or else attribute to ourselves a grasp of truth conditions which we could not recognize as obtaining only works if we grant his key premise: that "there is no . . . alternative account of what our grasp of the truth conditions of such sentences consists in" [other than the one which Dummett has proposed]. But we have seen that there is an alternative account of what our grasp of these truth conditions consists in. We need not hold that we grasp the truth conditions of, for example, statements about the past, by imagining what it would be to observe the past as we do the present. We can hold instead that we learn when to predicate "is true" of statements about the past by learning on what basis we are to count them as true.[7] That is, we can hold that we learn what counts as establishing past-tense statements as true by learning a *rule* which tells us the grounds upon which we affirm them—or a *convention* which tells us what it means to call a past-tense statement true. And once we conceive of learning the uses of "is true" as a matter of learning linguistic rules, the meaning we take our sentences to have is necessarily consistent with the use to which we put them. For we learn what it means to say that a past-tense statement p is true when we learn the criterion for judging its truth, that is, when we learn how to use the statement "p is true." Moreover, on an account of truth conditions as criteria, there is no problem of explaining what our grasp of the truth condition of a past-tense statement consists in: we will say that we learn what it is for it to be true by learning the criterion or the conventional rule which tells us when we may affirm its truth.

Something stronger can be said in favor of Wittgenstein's account of truth than that it does not require us to revise a practice which does not seem to entail any untoward philosophical commitments. We can also say that it provides a more faithful account of this existing practice than Dummett's antirealist picture. Recall that the antirealist is forced to deny that what makes a past-tense statement true is the fact that the sentence, when uttered in the past and in the present tense, was true. And, thus, he denies our intuition that we come to understand what makes statements about the past true by grasping the truth value link between past-tense statements and present-tense statements made in the past. For he holds that if something is true, it must be possible for us to know that it is true. And there is often no longer anything in virtue of which statements about the past are true, that is, there is often nothing left of the past. On Wittgenstein's account of truth, however, we have a way of upholding the truth value link between statements about the past made now and present-tense statements made in the past. We can make sense of our thought that our grasp of the truth value link forms part of our understanding of what makes past-tense statements true. What we can say is that the fact that we treated a statement as being true or false in the past and used it to express the type of certainty belonging to present-tense statements explains why we now treat the statement, in the past tense, as being true or false to express a different type of certainty. There is a causal link between our past treatment of a statement and our present treatment of it. That is, there is a causal link between our having predicated "is true" of a statement in the remote past and our predicating "is true" of a statement referring to the remote past. Our having treated a statement as being true or false in the remote past is one way in which we know the statement to be true or false when we use it in the present tense. And in learning how to use statements about the past what we come to understand is the link between differently tensed statements uttered at different times. The antirealist holds that treating statements about the remote past as being bivalent amounts to realism. And the antirealist then objects to this practice on the grounds that it amounts to treating a statement as being determinately true or false when there is no fact which we could recognize as obtaining in virtue of which it could be true. But we need not be realists to hold that statements about the past are determinately true or false. We can still hold that truth is internally related to our capacity for knowledge. But the traces of our previous knowledge, in legends and oral and written histories, are one way in which we can know about the past. Thus, Wittgenstein's account of truth provides us with a way of justifying our practice of acknowledging the truth value link between differently tensed statements without falling into the realist picture that the Wittgensteinian wants to avoid.[8]

## 6. Tensions between Wittgenstein and Dummett

We have seen that Dummett's attribution of antirealism to Wittgenstein cannot be supported by Wittgenstein's discussion of what Dummett calls undecidable statements. Far from lending itself to an antirealist reading, Wittgenstein's conception of meaning as use leads to a novel account of truth—and an account which avoids the truth value gaps that cause Dummett to reject a truth-conditional account of meaning. I will now argue that Dummett is led to misread Wittgenstein as being sympathetic to antirealism because of Dummett's misunderstanding of Wittgenstein's thought that meaning is use. Dummett's attribution of antirealism to Wittgenstein rests primarily on this dictum which Dummett cites in support of the manifestation criterion. Yet while Dummett makes some nominal use of the dictum, there is in fact a tension between an account of meaning as use and several assumptions on which he relies in his argument for antirealism. Specifically, I shall argue that "meaning is use" has implications which are at odds with both molecularism and revisionism. Therefore, Dummett's argument for semantic antirealism only seems plausible if we assume these departures from the thought behind "meaning is use." That is, Dummett is led to read antirealism into Wittgenstein because of his failure to recognize that "meaning is use" is incompatible with the assumptions which Dummett needs to back up his antirealism.

Recall that Dummett's argument for rejecting a truth-conditional account of our understanding of certain sentences presupposes that manifestation of that understanding must issue in a recognitional capacity. As Akeel Bilgrami and Simon Blackburn have argued, it is only if a speaker is required to manifest his grasp of a truth condition through his capacity to recognize it as obtaining when it obtains that it is impossible for him to manifest this understanding. However, if a speaker were allowed to manifest his grasp of a sentence's truth condition by using the sentence in theoretical explanations, we should have no ground for denying that he understood its truth condition.[1] Furthermore, Dummett's insistence that a speaker can only manifest his grasp of a truth condition through his capacity to recognize it as obtaining rests upon a narrow construal of what it is to understand a sentence. That is, it depends on what Blackburn terms "an empiricist equation between a conception of a state of affairs and a conception of our sensory access to that state of affairs." But, as Blackburn points out, linguistic understanding should not be construed so narrowly: we can also come to understand what it is for a state of affairs to obtain by an "indirect, theoretical description of the features or things involved." And so we should not insist that manifestation of a speaker's understanding must issue in a capacity to recognize a sentence's truth condition as obtaining when it obtains. We should allow that such understanding may also be manifested by various neighboring abilities such as,

> the ability to construct explanations dependent of the truth or falsity of the putatively undecidable sentence, the ability to tell why attempts at verification are blocked, the ability to tell things of related sorts, even if not this one, the ability to work out what else would be so if the sentence in question were undetectably true, the ability to embed the sentence in complex contexts and so on. (Blackburn 1989, p. 34)

For example, the statements "Dummett's only great-grandson will marry" and "Dummett's only great-grandson will always be a bachelor" are both undecidable because we are not at present in a position to determine their truth value. Yet if someone understood that both statements could not be true together, we should say that he had a grasp of what would make each of them true.[2] Therefore, we ought not to think of our grasp of the truth conditions of undecidable statements exclusively in terms of our capacity to tell whether they are true. We also show that we possess this understanding by showing that we understand what sort of thing would make them true, what would count as evidence for them, or how we would try to find out whether they were true.[3] It may in the end turn out that we cannot decide the truth value of a sentence such as "Jones was brave" where Jones, now dead, never encountered danger. It may be that there really is no evidence either way. But nevertheless, we have a conception of how we might find this sort of thing out. We understand what someone is doing when he checks Jones's high school and army records or asks about his trips to the dentist. And we are inclined to say that someone understands what would make such a sentence true insofar as we "can find method and intelligence in [his] researches . . . represent his aims to [ourselves] and appreciate his attempts to fulfill them." The fact that we know how to investigate the truth value of a sentence ought to suffice to attribute to ourselves a grasp of its truth condition. For it is our conception of what the truth value of a sentence consists in that gives our investigations their point. That is, we understand what counts as evidence of a statement because we have a grasp of what it is evidence *for*. Therefore, what we count as manifestation of a speaker's grasp of a truth condition should be expanded to include the abilities involved in investigating a sentence's truth value. And once our conception of manifestation has been broadened in this way, we have no basis for denying that a speaker understands something about the truth condition of a sentence which he treats as being true or false.

Dummett's demand that manifestation of our grasp of a truth condition must issue in a recognitional capacity springs from his belief that a meaning theory must be molecular. According to Dummett, the holistic view of meaning, whereby a sentence has meaning in the context of a whole language, is inadequate to the tasks of a theory of meaning. He argues that holism cannot account for language acquisition as "there can be nothing between not knowing a language at all and knowing it completely." Nor can it account for communication, for since no one knows an entire language, it seems to follow that no one understands the meaning of a sentence ("I can't know anything a man believes until I know (or guess) everything that he believes . . . so it becomes incomprehensible how anyone can tell another anything").[4]

And Dummett holds that if a meaning theory is to redress these deficiencies, it must give an account of what language mastery consists in which does not presuppose prior involvement in a linguistic community. A proper theory of language "must not make use of notions specifically related to the use of language (for instance the notion of assertion or that of communication) which it leaves unexplained."[5] In other words, Dummett argues, first, that if we want to discover what language mastery consists in, we must examine the way in which it was initially acquired. And, second, what counts as manifestation of this understanding cannot outrun the way in which it was initially acquired. Thus, he holds that since language is acquired cumulatively, one piece at a time, a speaker's understanding must be identified with his implicit knowledge of a language—that is, with a grasp of the lower level sentences which can be acquired without any prior linguistic competence and which could thus be grasped by someone who was not a member of a linguistic community. This, in turn, leads Dummett to hold that a speaker's understanding of his language must be manifested nonverbally, for example, by his capacity to recognize the truth condition of a sentence as obtaining when it obtains. As Dummett argues, if we allow what counts as manifestation of a speaker's understanding to issue in his capacity to give verbal explanations, we will be presupposing that he already has considerable linguistic ability. Thus, we will not have given an account of what language mastery consists in which distinguishes what a native speaker must know in order to speak his own language from what a foreigner must know in order to interpret another language.

Wittgenstein, however, would object to identifying what language mastery consists in with what Dummett terms "implicit knowledge." For he would argue that we cannot infer what language mastery itself consists in with the way in which language is initially acquired. According to Wittgenstein, understanding a language means being familiar with a multiplicity of language games which are involved in the activity of speaking a language. As he remarks, "To understand a sentence is to understand a language. To understand a language is to be a master of a technique" (*P.I.* #199). That is, to understand a language is to have a mastery of various uses to which language can be put, a mastery which enables a speaker to communicate. And our uses of language do not make sense in isolation from one another. They have content within a complex network of uses and customs which, taken together, compose a language. So the child who has reached the stage where he can be described as *using* language—that is, the stage at which his utterances are meaningful to himself as well as to others—must already be participating in many language games. For the speaker who can be described as *using* language must be aware of various possible contexts of utterance and various possible uses of language in order to recognize a legitimate move in a language game. Canfield remarks, "To utter a word in a given context is to engage in a language game. Language games are customs (*P.I.* #199). In learning to speak the child is acculturated: he acquires one by one the customs that make up a language."[6]

What language *is* is a collection of contexts, language games, or uses. The meaning of a word determines the contexts in which it is correct and incorrect to utter it; we say that an agent understands a word when he can distinguish between correct and incorrect uses of it. And, in learning the correct uses of a word, a child masters the proprieties of several inferences connecting its application to that of other words. For example, to learn the use of the word "red" is to learn to treat "This is red" as incompatible with "This is green," as following from "This is scarlet," and as entailing "This is colored." That is, as Robert Brandom argues, concepts are essentially inferentially articulated. To grasp a concept is to have a practical mastery of the inferences it is involved in. It is to be aware of its role in justifying some further attitudes and in ruling out others. And in order to grasp any one concept one must already have many other concepts. For to grasp a concept such as "red" is to master the proprieties of inferential moves that connect it to other concepts: those whose applicability follows from the applicability of the concept in question, and those whose applicability precludes or is precluded by it. So the notion of an autonomous language game is a radical mistake:[7] once a child can be described as making an intentional move in a language game, he must already be familiar with many others. This is not to say that the child must have mastered many concepts before he begins to utter words. We may of course acquire language one bit at a time. But once "light has begun to dawn over the whole" of what the child knows how to say—that is, once the child is making utterances which are meaningful to himself as well as to others (in contrast to those of a parrot which are meaningful only to others)—the child must be familiar with many different contexts of use. The molecularist who wishes to employ the slogan "meaning is use" forgets that a given use of language only makes sense within a particular context, that is, a particular language game. And this context in turn must be grasped within the broader context of a collection of customs. The meaning of a word is not its use as abstracted from a network of other uses—that is, from the language in which it is used. Rather, it is its use within a complex form of life. Therefore, if we want an account of what language mastery consists in, we should not turn our attention to the way it is initially acquired. For to *fully* understand a sentence is to understand a language. Wittgenstein's remark at *P.I.* #32 illustrates this point:

> Someone coming into a strange country will sometimes learn the language of the inhabitants from ostensive definitions that they give him; and he will often have to guess the meaning of these definitions, and he will sometimes guess right and sometimes guess wrong. And now I think we can say: Augustine describes the learning of human language as if the child came into a strange country and did not understand the language of the country: that is, as if it already had a language, only not this one. Or again: as if the child could think, only not yet speak. And "think" would here mean something like "talk to itself."

Wittgenstein's suggestion here is that whereas the foreigner, who has already acquired the concepts being ostensively defined in a foreign tongue, will sometimes be able to make correct educated guesses, the preverbal child who has not yet acquired *any* language will be completely unable to make sense of ostensive definitions. For the preverbal child lacks the semantic categories with which to make sense of new words. In order for a speaker to understand what kind of word is being defined, he must be familiar with the uses of different kinds of words in language. And for this he must be familiar with a multiplicity of different language games, in which he learns to participate as he learns a language (*P.I.* #30, #31). To understand a word or sentence is to know how to use it (*P.I.* #1, #29). And to be able to use a word or a sentence is to be capable of recognizing the contexts in which it is appropriate to utter it.[8] Therefore, the project of giving an account of what a speaker must know to speak a language as distinct from what a foreigner must know in order to interpret one is ultimately misguided. A speaker's knowledge must not be identified with what Dummett terms his implicit knowledge, that is, with the sentences he can acquire without any prior linguistic ability. Rather, a speaker's knowledge must be identified with what he knows how to do after he has mastered a language. This is not to deny that language is acquired one fragment at a time and cumulatively. But the way in which language is initially acquired is irrelevant to what language mastery consists in. As Akeel Bilgrami puts this point,

> The holist need not deny that we in fact acquire language mastering some one fragment and then some other and so on, nor even which fragment we are more likely to begin with

('tables' and 'chairs' before 'mass' and 'unconscious'). She
cannot deny this because these are manifestly facts. [But what
she can say is] that these facts are not relevant to the tasks of
a theory of meaning which is only concerned with specifying
what knowledge suffices for someone to be the master of a
language; and that this specification need not mirror the process by which one came to be a master. The facts, therefore,
have no philosophical significance. The holist only needs to say
that though one, of course, learns a language by learning one
fragment and then another, in learning an initial fragment one
has not *fully* mastered it, and will only learn it fully if one learns
others. In learning the others, one may not only add to but
even revise one's understanding of the initial fragment.[9]

Clearly, what a speaker who has mastered a language understands
by a sentence goes far beyond what a child who is still in the process
of becoming a language user understands by it. The linguistic behavior
of the child who is just starting to engage in primitive language games
can be described in strictly causal terms. For example, when we train
a child to turn his head in the direction we are pointing when we say
the word "Look!," we resist saying that the child *understands* the word
or that we have *explained its meaning* to him.[10] We say instead that he is
*reacting* and that we have trained him to respond to our gesture, much
as we might train an animal (cf. *B.B.* p. 77). However, as the child
begins to participate in more complex language games, it ceases to be
possible to explain his linguistic behavior in purely mechanical terms.
For the different kinds of uses that words have demand increasingly
complex accounts of an agent's behavior. Once a speaker has reached
the stage of communicational complexity where it makes sense to speak
of language use, his behavior requires intentional and normative concepts for its correct description and explanation. The point here is not
a developmental one, but a grammatical one:[11] behavioral criteria must
be satisfied before we can speak of teaching—that is, of giving explanations of meaning—rather than of training. That is, there must be
sufficient complexity in an agent's behavior in order for us to speak of
teaching him. Or, to put the point another way, an agent's behavior
must exhibit a certain degree of complexity in order for us to attribute
understanding to him. And, as Stuart Shanker argues, this is why we do
not say that a dog has the concept of "mealtime" because he salivates
to the sound of a bell: "it is not that we lack sufficient evidence to know
what the dog is thinking, but that the language game played with 'time'
demands far greater behavioral complexity than has been displayed by

the dog in order to describe it as possessing even a primitive version of the concept."[12] In other words, it is part of the grammar of the concept of "speaking a language" that we describe this activity in normative terms. To speak of "the meaning of an expression" is to speak of the ways in which it is *correct* or incorrect to use it. And, thus, to say that a speaker *understands* the meaning is to say that he can *distinguish* between correct and incorrect uses of it.[13] Therefore, the language *master* differs from the language *learner* in that the master has arrived in what Wilfred Sellars has termed the "space of giving and asking for reasons": he understands what makes a given utterance correct or incorrect and can justify his use of it.

For this reason, what counts as manifestation of a speaker's understanding cannot be modeled on the way it was initially acquired. And in particular we must not insist that manifestation of his knowledge of a truth condition must issue in a (nonverbal) recognitional capacity. Instead, we must allow manifestation of a speaker's knowledge to issue in his capacity to perform verbally. And his knowledge of a truth condition must issue in a capacity, *inter alia*, to state it. And once manifestation of a speaker's knowledge is allowed to issue in the stating response, then the statements Dummett classifies as having "recognition-transcendent truth conditions" no longer appear undecidable. For when a speaker is asked what the truth condition of a statement is, he can give the criterion whereby he determines the truth value of the statement. That is, he can give the relevant rule he uses for determining the truth value of the statement, which is dependent on the language game to which the statement belongs and which is his way of determining its truth value.

Dummett's case that we cannot understand the truth conditions of certain sentences presupposes that we must demonstrate our understanding by recognizing these truth conditions. It presupposes that we cannot demonstrate our understanding through our capacity to formulate them verbally or in any other manner which would require more linguistic competence than we had in our initial stages of language acquisition. This constraint on what can count as manifestation of linguistic understanding springs, in turn, from Dummett's molecularism. More precisely, it springs from his desire to give an account of what language mastery consists in which does not presuppose any linguistic competence or any prior involvement in a linguistic community. But this project ought to appear misguided to a proponent of the dictum that "meaning is use."[14] The use of a word is, after all, its use within a whole language, that is, within a complex network of other uses. So in order for a speaker to be described as using language (as distinct from making very primitive utterances), he must already have competence in that language. As John McDowell remarks, "[i]f we insist on eliminating dependence on prior involvement in forms of life, then we eliminate the very possibility of understanding."[15]

We can make the further point that if we accept the holism entailed by an account of meaning as use, we cannot justify rejecting a community's acceptance of a given inference as evidence that the community has a grasp of the truth conditions of the statements involved. Rather, if a community accepts an inference which presupposes the bivalence of a statement, we will be compelled to take whatever content the community assigns to calling the statement true or false as constitutive of the statement's truth value. For if we hold that the meaning of a word is its intersubjective use, or that a fragment of language has meaning only within the context of an entire language, then our sentences will have whatever meaning our use confers on them. That is, a statement will have meaning in virtue of our use, and an inference will be valid in virtue of our treatment of it as valid. For to hold that meaning is use is to be committed to conventionalism, that is, to the view that there is no extralinguistic standard by reference to which an inference can be said to be valid or a statement can be called bivalent. On this view, therefore, a community's acceptance of an inference presupposing the bivalence of a statement must be seen as a sufficient reason to hold that the statement is decidable. For the dictum that meaning is use forces on us an account of truth conditions as criteria rather than as correspondence with possibly recognition-transcendent facts. This is not, of course, to say that Dummett could not advance an independent argument to justify constructing a semantic theory which would be capable of leveling criticisms at a practice. But it is not open to him to argue that semantic antirealism is implicit in the dictum that meaning is use if he also wishes to claim that a theory of meaning should be revisionist. For "meaning is use" is in considerable tension with molecularism and revisionism.

Given that the assumptions behind semantic antirealism conflict with an account of meaning as use, it is fair to ask what Dummett's commitment to the dictum amounts to. Generally speaking, he writes as though it amounts to the view that meaning is not private, that understanding must be manifestable. But the primary thought expressed by "meaning is use" is not that meaning is social and cannot be private, but rather that language has meaning in virtue of our intersubjective use of it. The thesis that meaning cannot be private and the thesis that language is essentially intersubjective are not equivalent. Some philosophers have been committed to the first thesis without holding the second one,[16] although the second claim is logically prior to the first. And if one does reject the second claim, as Dummett does through his commitment to molecularism and revisionism, one will have no way of arguing that meaning cannot be private.[17] Why, then, does Dummett want to maintain that a practice may stand in need of revision? That is, why, if he accepts one implication of "meaning is use," does he reject the conventionalism that is also implied by it? Molecularism and revisionism are of course connected in Dummett's argument: if we are to be able to criticize our practice of treating certain sentences as bivalent, then we must take a sentence as saying something on its own. For the antirealist/revisionist wants to be able to say that a sentence is not determinately true or false if "no procedure is known for making a strong empirical case for its truth or falsity."[18] And if, as W. V. O. Quine says, a sentence does not come with its own bundle of empirical content but faces the tribunal of experience only as part of a corporate body, then no truth value assignment of any sentence is ever mandatory in the light of experience.[19] What is less clear is Dummett's initial motivation for revisionism; why does he want a meaning theory to be able to criticize a practice? The answer to this question is never given explicitly. But Dummett sometimes writes as though his revisionism springs from a commitment to something like the realist conception of meaning associated with logical atomism. Consider the following passage:

> A sentence is a representation of some facet of reality. . . . The theory of meaning, which lies at the foundation of the whole of philosophy, attempts to explain how we represent reality by means of language. It does so by giving a model for the content of each sentence, its representative power. Holism is . . . the denial that a theory of meaning is possible. On a holistic view, no model for the individual content of a sentence can be given: we cannot grasp the representative power of any one sentence save by a complete grasp of the linguistic properties underlying our use of the entire language, and when we have such a grasp of this whole, there is no way in which this can be systematized so as to give us a clear view of the contribution of any particular part of the apparatus . . . we are part of the mechanism and cannot view it from the outside. (*T.O.E.*, p. 309)

The view of meaning that Dummett is putting forth here bears an obvious affinity to the picture theory of the *Tractatus*. Just as Wittgenstein held there that a proposition presents a state of affairs, so Dummett maintains that a sentence represents some segment of reality. He equates the content of a sentence with its representative power. And thus he holds as well that what makes a sentence true or false is its agreement or lack of agreement with what it represents. That is, more precisely, he adheres to the traditional Fregean view that meaning along with whatever is nonconventional (such as "facts" or "evidence") determines the semantic values of our statements. And he holds that, as long as we appreciate the facts, the semantic values we assign to our statements will coincide with their "true" semantic values.[20] Just as Wittgenstein held in the *Tractatus* that a proposition is true if and only if the state of affairs it presents obtains, so Dummett remarks that "the question as to the nature of reality is also the question what is the appropriate notion of truth for sentences in our language, or again, how we represent reality by means of language" (*T.O.E.*, p. 314). And elsewhere he writes that

> Metaphysics attempts to describe the most general structural features of reality . . . by expressing the structural features of . . . our language as structural features of the world about which we think and talk. More particularly, a semantic theory will tell us what, in general, makes a statement of one or another kind true, if it is true: in virtue of what it is capable of being true. . . . Viewed in one kind of way, a thesis about what, in general, makes a statement of a given kind true is a semantic thesis, determining the type of content attaching to a statement of that kind. Viewed in another way, it is a metaphysical thesis telling us what is the substance of a certain sector of reality: what kinds of thing, or better, what facts, constitute that reality.[21]

Now only someone who adheres to a realist view of meaning—and who, accordingly, sees the meaning-theoretical task as one of explaining our assignments of semantic value—will want a semantic theory to be capable of being revisionist. For only someone who thinks that sentences have meaning and truth value in virtue of *representing reality* will think we must be able to *view a practice from the outside* to see if it is in need of revision. The holist, who construes the meaning of a sentence as its use within a language instead of as its representative power, will not see the necessity of "getting outside the [linguistic] mechanism and viewing it from the outside." For since the holist thinks that a sentence has content in virtue of its use, there is no type of consideration independent of a practice that could tell us that we must revise a practice. As Kenneth Winkler puts this point, "holism calls into question the distinction between fact and convention upon which Dummett's conception of the meaning-theoretical task depends."[22] Here there is an analogy between Dummett's thought that in order to know what would make a past-tense statement true, we must survey the past from a perspective outside of the time sequence, and the thought that a language must be subject to criticism from a perspective outside of a practice: Only someone who is already committed to realism will think we must be able to get outside a practice in order to judge its correctness. Thus, it is not surprising that Dummett misreads Wittgenstein as being sympathetic to antirealism nor that Dummett puts forth an argument for this which contradicts the view that meaning is use. For there is some evidence that Dummett is less sympathetic to Wittgenstein's later conception of meaning than he is to the early Wittgenstein's picture theory.[23]

## 7. Semantic Antirealism Is Inconsistent

I have argued that Dummett's attribution of semantic antirealism to Wittgenstein is a misinterpretation; that it presupposes a realist account of truth which Wittgenstein rejected and, further, that it depends on a molecular view of meaning which is at odds with an account of meaning as use. I will now argue for a stronger claim: that, independently of whether it can attributed to Wittgenstein, semantic antirealism in itself is not a consistent position. I shall then suggest that, once we have rejected a realist account of truth, Wittgenstein's view of truth is the one which we should accept.

To see why semantic antirealism is inconsistent, let us re-examine Dummett's argument that statements about the remote past are not determinately true or false. Now Dummett holds first (Principle C) that it is part of our concept of truth that if something is true, there must be some segment of reality in virtue of which it is true. That is, he is committed to some form of a realist/correspondence theory of truth. And, second, he holds (Principle K) that if something is true, it must be possible for us to know that it is true. That is, he is committed to some form of a verificationist theory of truth. There is a tension between realism and verificationism,[1] and it comes out in the following way: because he is committed to Principle C, Dummett holds that the truth of statements about the remote past consists in their correspondence to a segment of reality which is now no longer existent. Thus, he holds that finding out whether these statements are true must involve surveying the past as we do the present, from some perspective outside of the time sequence. And, because he is committed to Principle K, Dummett holds that because we *cannot* survey the past, statements about the remote past do not have truth conditions. As he argues, since it is impossible for us to observe the past from a perspective outside of the time sequence, there is nothing which the truth value of statements referring to the remote past could consist in. However, if one were really committed to the thought that if something is true, it must be possible for us to know that it is true, then our inability to survey the past ought not to matter to whether statements about the past have truth conditions. For if we think of truth as being related to our capacity for knowledge, we will not hold that the truth of past-tense statements consists in their correspondence with the past. And, thus, we will not hold that finding out whether they are true must involve surveying the past from a perspective outside of the time sequence. Instead, we will say that the truth value of statements about the past consists in whatever evidence we take as decisive for establishing them as true or false. And we will construe finding out whether they are true in terms of examining this evidence. That is to say: if we adopt a verificationist account of truth (as Principle K suggests) we will not construe finding out whether a past-tense statement is true or false in a way which would transcend our ability to determine its truth value. For if we really hold that if something is true, it must be possible for us to know that it is true, then if a certain type of fact is such that we could never in principle determine whether it obtained, then we will not consider this type of fact as the type of thing in which the truth value of a statement consists. We will have to keep in mind here that the predicate "is true" does not apply to facts, but rather to statements and beliefs. We do not say that *facts* are true or false, but that statements are true or false.

Wittgenstein's account of truth is to be preferred to semantic antirealism. For unlike Dummett's view, Wittgenstein's is consistent with the motivation for rejecting realism. Wittgenstein argues that the realist cannot give content to what he says is his concept of truth. The realist construes the truth of a sentence as its correspondence with a fact that makes it true. And he thinks that some sentences are made true by facts which transcend our capacity for knowledge. Thus, through his commitment to the idea of transcendent truth, the realist is attempting to attach a meaning to "is true" which outruns the use to which we could put the predicate. For on his account of truth, the truth predicate would apply to sentences for which we could have no way of determining their truth value.

Wittgenstein holds that we must abandon the correspondence account of what makes a true sentence true. For the concept of truth that it commits us to goes beyond what we could come to grasp through our use of language. We acquire the concept of truth by learning to use the word "true" in our language, that is, by applying the predicate to actual sentences. And if the meaning of "is true" were such that we could have no way of telling when it applied to a sentence, then the word could not have any use in language. Here there is an analogy with the beetle in the box: if we should have no way of knowing what sort of thing to call a beetle, the word "beetle" could not play any role in language. And if part of the meaning of "true" were such that we could have no way of telling when to apply it to certain sentences, then whatever was supposed to correspond to this aspect of its meaning could not play any role in language. If we want to find out what our concept of truth amounts to, we must examine the role that the truth predicate plays in our discourse. We must examine the circumstances in which we use the word "true." And whenever we apply the truth predicate to a sentence, we have a way of determining its truth value. That is, we have a criterion of its truth, which is an appropriate test of the type of statement it is, and which counts as a way of telling whether it is true. Our concept of truth is internally related to our capacity for knowledge—to our capacity to learn of the truth values of our statements. And, thus, it makes sense, once we have rejected the realist picture of truth, to hold that truth conditions are determined by our criteria for judging truth values. To adopt Dummett's line and deny that bivalence holds for certain statements that we treat as true or false is still to be committed to realism.

Wittgenstein's account of truth goes beyond antirealism in rejecting the metaphysics of transcendent truth. And it allows us to see both sides of the realist/antirealist debate as part of the same metaphysical tradition. Antirealists follow Wittgenstein in rejecting the idea of transcendent truth, yet they remain very much implicitly committed to the realist view of truth that lies behind it. Therefore, in rejecting realism, they merely replace it with another view based on the same metaphysical assumption. Wittgenstein's more radical critique of realism sees the realist's view of truth as untenable. He replaces it with an account of truth that is free of metaphysical assumptions: that, as there is nothing more to meaning than use, there is nothing more to our concept of truth than we can grasp through our use of statements that we treat as being true or false.

# PART III

# Why a Revisionist Account
# of Truth?

It is part of our understanding of the concept of knowledge—or as Wittgenstein would say, it is part of the grammar of "knowing"—that knowledge entails the truth of what is known. An epistemology which denies the entailment will accordingly seem to most of us to be one that we should reject.[1] We have seen that Wittgenstein held that truth conditions are determined by criteria, that is, by conventional ways of finding out whether our statements are true. Many commentators, beginning with Rogers Albritton, have assumed that criteria are defeasible. That is, they have held that it is possible for the criterion of a claim to be satisfied and for the criterially governed claim to be false. Thus, they have held that criteria determine what counts as good evidence for a statement that some state of affairs obtains, but do not strictly define what it is for that state of affairs to obtain. For since they hold that it is possible for a criterion to be satisfied and a criterially governed object to be absent, they take the criteria of our various statements as falling short of being decisive for establishing them as true. That is, they hold that our criteria provide "necessary evidence" or "noninductive evidence" for our statements, but fall short of being decisive for establishing their truth. And, thus, they argue that criteria should be taken as determining the conditions under which we are justified in asserting our statements rather than as determining their truth conditions. However, Crispin Wright has argued that if criterially based knowledge does not entail the truth of what is known, then criteria cannot provide the requisite notion of entitlement for our assertions and hence cannot play any role in a theory of knowledge or of meaning. And John McDowell has gone in the other direction and argued that since defeasibility is incompatible with the thought that knowledge entails the truth of what is known, then if a criterially based epistemology is to preserve this thought, it must interpret criteria as being similar to realist truth conditions.

I will argue that criteria ought to be taken as providing an alternative and novel conception of truth conditions. They are not to be taken as realist truth conditions, nor are they to be taken as conditions which justify our assertions but fall short of establishing them as true. As I will argue, the resistance to seeing criteria as the basis of a novel conception of truth conditions springs from a refusal to take our uses of "is true" as relevant to our conception of a truth condition. Or to put the point more broadly, it springs from a refusal to take our uses of "is true" as relevant to the concept of truth or to the meaning of "is true." For it is, in part, this refusal that leads to the view that criteria are defeasible. But, as I will argue, once we acknowledge the relevance of the way in which we use a given sentence in the context of predicating "is true" of it to our conception of its truth condition, we will not hold that we treat any sentence's criterion as being defeasible. What we will hold is that we treat our criteria as being *in principle* revisable. The difference between defeasibility and revisability is significant enough that once we interpret criteria in the latter way, it is open to us to take them as providing truth conditions. And an epistemology based on criteria allows us to uphold the thought that knowledge entails the truth of what is known, albeit in an unusual way which calls for what I will argue is a necessary and justified revision in our traditional picture of truth.

In chapters 8 and 9, I distinguish criteria from defeasible assertibility conditions and realist truth conditions. In chapter 10, I show how we might reject the argument for the view of criteria as providing defeasible, necessary evidence. In chapter 11, I discuss how a criterial change can take place within a community, and I outline the revisionist account of truth which follows from the fact that we treat criteria both as providing truth conditions and as being in principle revisable. Finally, I consider some objections to the account of truth put forth here, and I contrast the Wittgensteinian view with an alternative approach to avoiding a transcendent account of truth. I then argue that once we accept the arguments that truth is an epistemological concept, we should be prepared to reject any view which makes our concept of truth transcend our current capacity for knowledge. Instead, we should take the meaning of "is true" as being determined by the conditions under which we are *correct* in calling a statement true. And what determines the conditions under which it is *correct* to predicate "is true" of our statements should be taken as the criteria and conventions that we use for determining our statements' truth values.

## 8. Criteria and Justification Conditions

In his "Second Thoughts about Criteria," Crispin Wright expresses skepticism about whether criteria can play the role he had previously envisioned in a semantic theory based on assertibility conditions. Formerly, Wright had held that criteria might provide an alternative to realist truth conditions in an account of what it is to treat a sentence as assertible.[1] For criteria would be taken as providing necessarily good evidence for a statement in virtue of a convention. That is, a criterion would be taken as a good ground on which to make an assertion, a ground which would have this status by virtue of convention or definition. So we would be justified in claiming to know some statement p on recognition that the criterion of the statement was satisfied. Yet at the same time, it would be part of our notion of a criterially based assertion that the best evidence that we could have might fall short of being conclusive. That is, it would always remain a possibility that the criterion of some claim might be satisfied although the criterially governed claim was false. For example, we might claim to know that someone was in pain on the basis of his pain behavior, having learned to treat pain behavior as necessarily good evidence for pain ascriptions. Yet it would always be possible that in an exceptional case someone might exhibit pain behavior without being in pain; he or she might merely be pretending. So criteria would fall short of providing conditions which establish criterially governed claims as true. They would instead provide conditions which merely justify us in asserting our statements. And thus the semantic antirealist had hoped that the notion of a criterion could provide the basis of a suitable alternative to a realist truth-conditional theory of meaning. He had held that the notion might provide the basis of an account of what it means to assert an undecidable sentence, which would be consistent with the use to which we put such sentences. That is, it could explain how we learn to affirm and deny these sentences without attributing to ourselves a grasp of truth conditions which we could not recognize as obtaining. And, thus, it could account for the meaning of our statements' assertibility conditions without making our grasp of them impossible to manifest in our use, which the semantic antirealist is anxious to avoid doing.

In "Second Thoughts," however, Wright thinks that there are insurmountable problems with the notion of a criterion which preclude it from meeting the requirements of an antirealist meaning theory. He argues that the very feature of being defeasible or of "falling short of being truth conditions" which had made criteria so attractive to the assertibility conditions theorist will make it impossible for criteria to play any role in a semantic theory. For if it is part of the concept of a criterially based assertion that the satisfaction of a criterion is always consistent with a criterially governed claim's proving false, we will not take ourselves to be justified in making assertions on the basis of criteria. That is, it is part of the concept of making an assertion that we assume responsibility for what we claim; we do not assert a statement with an open mind about subsequent defeat. Thus, Wright concludes that, because they are defeasible, criteria cannot provide conditions under which we take ourselves as being justified in asserting the sentences whose truth conditions transcend our ability to verify them. And he holds that if the defeasibility feature is waived, criteria will not be interestingly different from realist truth conditions.[2]

Wright's argument for this conclusion presupposes a particular interpretation of criteria. It presupposes accepting certain features which he attributes to criteria as being "cardinal features" of them. And whether we are obliged to accept Wright's conclusion about criteria ultimately depends on whether we accept the view of criteria that it rests upon. We shall see that Wright's claim that "orthodoxy in the interpretation of criteria" attributes these features to them is an exaggeration. But the view that Wright is committed to is certainly one that is widely held. Thus it is useful to examine the role that the features he attributes to criteria play in his argument that criteria cannot provide an alternative to realist truth conditions in an account of what it means to assert a sentence. For by doing so, we will come to understand a common source of the traditional resistance to treating Wittgenstein's concept of a criterion as the basis of a novel conception of a truth condition. And we can then see how a Wittgensteinian might overcome these objections.

According to Wright, the following are the essential features of criteria:[3]

1. that recognition of satisfaction of criteria for p confers skeptic-proof knowledge that p (the knowledge feature);
2. that p's criteria determine necessarily good evidence for p and thereby fix its content (the meaning feature);
3. that the satisfaction of a criterion will always be a public matter;
4. that to know of the satisfaction of criteria for p is always consistent with having or discovering further information whose effect is that the claim that p is not justified after all.

Wright argues that the defeasibility feature of criteria cannot be made to harmonize with either the knowledge feature or the meaning feature. And, thus, the notion of a criterion cannot provide an accurate account of our practice of making knowledge claims. Or to put the point another way, criteria cannot give content to the use to which we put assertions. Thus, criteria cannot provide the conditions under which we assert that our statements are true nor the conditions under which we claim to know them. He presents this case in the following way.

He first points out that our practice of making knowledge claims is based on our conception of knowledge as entailing the truth of what is known. When we claim to know some statement p, we are vouching for the truth of that statement. That is, we take ourselves to be understood as saying that our knowledge claim is guaranteed *correct*. And thus, when we claim to know that p, we must have a conclusive basis on which to claim to know it. But if the criteria of our statements are taken as being open to defeat, then a knowledge claim made upon recognizing the satisfaction of a criterion will not be made on a conclusive basis. It will be made on the basis of something which is consistent with our obtaining further information according to which our claim is not justified. So knowledge that criteria are satisfied cannot amount to knowledge that p, as we normally think about knowledge. Thus, the notion of a criterion cannot serve as the basis of an account of making knowledge claims. For it cannot give content to our concept of knowledge as guaranteeing truth.

Wright suggests that the proponent of criteria could make the following emendation in the knowledge feature: he could argue that knowledge that the criterion of a statement is satisfied is not supposed to constitute knowledge that the claim in question is *true*. Rather, the recognition that the criterion of a statement was satisfied would tell us when we were justified in asserting it; it would tell us when we were *entitled* to claim knowledge of it. And it would be part of our concept of a criterially based knowledge claim that any such claim might have to be withdrawn. That is, it might be argued that what constitutes the truth of a knowledge claim is just the state of information of the claimant at the time of making it. And if he should subsequently acquire information in light of which he could no longer claim to know that p, his original claim would "no more be contradicted than would yesterday's claim, "It is raining" by today's assertion of "It is not raining." In other words, we might "identify the content of the claim to know that p with . . . the claim that one's present state of information includes awareness of satisfaction of criteria for p and of no consideration defeating the warrant for p which that supplies." Or, to put the point another way, we could deny that the content of a knowledge claim is given by an explanation of the truth conditions of what is claimed. Instead, we could hold that the content of such claims is given by "explaining the criteria for making them and the conditions under which those criteria should be considered defeated and the statements withdrawn."

Wright denies that emending the knowledge feature along these lines makes the notion of criterially based knowledge more coherent. First of all, it leaves it unclear what knowledge is being taken to be. Or, to put the point another way, it leaves it unclear what is supposed to constitute knowledge that a given claim is true. On the hypothesis that criteria are defeasible, recognition of the satisfaction of a criterion cannot constitute this knowledge; criteria and truth-conferring facts are distinct. And this poses a dilemma: in a case where an agent is said to know that p and makes a justified knowledge claim on the basis of a criterion, either the truth-conferring fact of p lies within his cognitive reach or it does not. If it does, then one can ask, "what is the point of this convention, when provided the subject does know that p, a further investigation will disclose a state of affairs which *constitutes* the fact?" And on the other hand, if the truth-conferring fact lies beyond the subject's cognitive reach when he makes this claim, then the skeptic can ask why the adoption of a convention is supposed to provide a reason for claiming the existence of a distinct state of affairs.

The more serious objection to the proposal is that because it calls for a revision in our concept of knowledge as a skeptic-proof epistemic state, it cannot provide an accurate account of our practice of making knowledge claims. And, therefore, emending the knowledge feature of criteria in this way will not make criteria more useful to the assertibility conditions theorist. For if criteria are taken as defeasible, they cannot give content to the use to which we actually put our knowledge claims. The fact is that we do normally think of knowledge as a stable, truth-entailing state. We cannot make sense of saying that we no longer know what we did know. And therefore it is built into our practice of making knowledge claims that we do not responsibly make them with an open mind about subsequent defeat. To suppose that one had full reason for making an assertion yet no reason to discount the possibility of its being defeated would be inconsistent with our practice of making knowledge claims. For a knowledge claim is a claim about the future; in claiming to know, we seek to transfer information that can be acted on. And as Wright remarks, "It is impossible to see what it would be to put the assertions of others to practical use if the convention was that no expectations were licensed." Thus, explaining the content of knowledge claims in terms of conditions which justify us in making them rather than in terms of their truth conditions does not allow us to make more sense of claiming knowledge on the basis of criteria. For a notion of correctness *as distinct* from correctness relative to a state of information is implicit even in the notion of a justified assertion.[4] But because criteria are defeasible, the notion of a criterially based assertion cannot give content to our practice of *treating* knowledge claims made by ourselves and others as being guaranteed correct. Thus, criteria cannot be regarded as providing the grounds on which we make such claims.

Wright makes the related point that because criteria are defeasible, they cannot be regarded as determining *a priori* good grounds or necessary evidence for our statements. And, therefore, a criterion cannot be regarded as providing the conditions which determine a statement's correct use. In other words, the defeasibility feature of criteria is incompatible with what Wright terms the meaning feature: criteria cannot provide assertibility conditions or conditions which justify our assertions. And hence, criteria cannot provide an alternative account of meaning to the realist truth-conditional account.

The antirealist's motivation for wanting to replace the realist truth-conditional account of meaning is his demand that understanding be manifestable. That is, he holds that, "[t]he most one can ask, if someone is to *show* that he understands a particular statement is that he displays . . . a practical grasp of the distinction between states of affairs that may reasonably be taken to warrant its assertion and states of affairs that may not." And the antirealist holds as well that the putative truth conditions of certain sentences, such as those referring to others' inner states, would transcend our ability to recognize them. For the process of verifying such sentences would outrun our ability to learn of their truth value. Thus, he argues that to say that the assertibility conditions of such sentences amount to truth conditions is to misdescribe their meaning. For if a sentence's truth condition transcends our ability to recognize it as obtaining when it obtains, its truth condition can play no role in how we come to use the sentence in the context of affirming and denying it. Accordingly, the antirealist wants to explain the meaning of such problematic sentences by reference to conditions of warranted assertion whose obtaining is not sufficient for their truth. He wants to regard these sentences as being associated with assertibility conditions which are treated both as having that status a priori and as being defeasible. For he holds, first, that "in order for an expression to have a determinate meaning at all, it must on some level be a matter of convention what its correct use consists in: "any . . . empirical investigation into whether it is correctly used in a particular case presupposes such a convention." Secondly, he holds that assertibility conditions must be regarded as defeasible because "the circumstance that standard assertion conditions of a statement were not sufficient for its truth would have to be manifestable in the *use* of the statement." And the only way in which that could be manifest is if the obtaining of those conditions were, under further circumstances, "acknowledged as insufficient for the correct assertibility of the statement." In other words, the only way we could manifest our knowledge that our best grounds for asserting a statement might fail to be conclusive is by treating those grounds as being fallible indicators. Criteria had seemed to be good candidates for providing such assertibility conditions. For criterial rules are supposed to determine what counts as good evidence for a statement in virtue of conventions of language. For example, it is supposed to be true in virtue of a rule of language that pain behavior is necessary evidence that someone is in pain. Yet at the same time, the criterial relation is supposed to be weaker than entailment. And thus it is supposed to be part of our conception of criterially governed claims such as pain ascriptions that we recognize the grounds upon which we make them as fallible.

Wright contends, however, that a criterion's being defeasible is in fact incompatible with its being taken as providing necessarily good evidence for a statement. For if a criterion is defeasible, it may be defeated. And if it is defeated often enough, we will not take it as a ground on which we are justified in making assertions. As Wright puts it, "no type of ground, even one conventionally associated with P can be *necessarily* 'good evidence' if it is regarded as a defeasible ground for . . . it may be defeated . . . so frequently that, bearing in mind the consequential character of any assertion of P, one would rightly become reluctant to assert P on its basis." Thus, he concludes that criteria cannot provide the basis of the hoped-for alternative to a realist theory of meaning.

What are we to make of Wright's argument that criteria provide no viable alternative to realist truth conditions? First of all, we should notice that it presupposes the necessary evidence, or, as it is sometimes called, the noninductive evidence view of criteria. That is, it presupposes the interpretation of criteria put forth by Lycan, Baker, and others which holds that the criterial relation is a new sort of logical relation which is "stronger than induction, but weaker than entailment." For it is on this interpretation that criteria are not decisive for establishing the truth of criterially governed claims. Wright argues that criteria cannot be an alternative to realist truth conditions because the former cannot provide the basis of an account of the use to which we put assertions. He argues that because criteria are defeasible, they cannot provide conditions under which we take ourselves as justified in making assertions. For defeasible criteria cannot give content to the consequential character that we treat assertions as having. And, in his overview of the features of criteria, Wright presents defeasibility as a separate, independent characteristic. In fact, however, the concept of defeasibility is built right in to the meaning feature—namely, that the criteria for p determine *necessarily good evidence for* p, but fall short of being decisive for establishing p as true. And, as we shall see, this is not the only way to interpret the criterial relation; there is another view according to which criteria are not defeasible. This is the defining criteria view, originally proposed by Albritton and defended by Canfield. On this view, if X is a criterion for Y, then it is true in virtue of a rule of language, convention, or definition that if X obtains, Y obtains. That is, a criterion for X is a grammatically or logically determined ground or reason for the obtaining of X. These conventional links between criteria and criterially governed statements are a human creation; they may be adopted ad hoc and be of short duration. And because a convention is adopted for a particular purpose, any given criterial rule is only applicable within a limited context. That is, as Canfield argues, it is not the case that a phenomenon which we treat as criterion for some claim is always a criterion. The circumstances have to be appropriate for us to apply a criterial rule before we can say that the criterion of a claim is *met*. But when the criterion of a claim is met, this is decisive for establishing that a criterially governed claim is true.

Wright argues that criteria cannot be taken as warranted assertibility conditions because they cannot provide the basis on which we make our knowledge claims. For if criteria are defeasible, then the recognition that the criterion of a statement is satisfied cannot constitute knowledge that the statement is true. And if the satisfaction of P's criterion does not constitute knowledge that P is true, it cannot entitle us to claim knowledge—we do not feel justified in making knowledge claims when we feel that they may be overturned. But the view that recognition of the satisfaction of P's criterion does *not* constitute knowledge that P is true presupposes acceptance of Wright's meaning feature. It presupposes that criteria are not decisive for establishing the truth of criterially governed claims. But if we accept the interpretation that says that criteria *are* decisive, then it is open to us to take criteria as a basis on which we make knowledge claims. For on this view, someone who has recognized that the criterion that p is met will have recognized the truth-conferring fact. And, as the satisfaction of the criterion of p will be taken as establishing the truth of p, we would indeed take ourselves as justified in asserting p on this basis. Thus, if we adopt the "defining criteria" view in favor of the necessary evidence view of criteria, it is open to us to take criteria as providing conditions which justify us in making assertions—or, to put the point another way, which justify us in predicating "is true" of our sentences. And if—as I will argue that we ought to—we think of truth conditions as determined by linguistic rules which tell us what we are currently justified in taking as true, then it is open to us to take criteria as providing a novel conception of truth conditions.

I have suggested a way in which criteria can be taken as providing an alternative to realist truth conditions in an account of what it means to treat a sentence as being assertible, that is, as being the sort of thing which can figure in knowledge claims, affirmations, and denials. As I have shown, it is not obviously necessary to take criteria as being *either* defeasible assertibility conditions *or else* as being realist truth conditions. Instead, we can take criteria as the basis of a novel conception of a truth condition which links the concept of a sentence's truth condition to our grounds for predicating "is true" of it or to the way that the sentence is used. I would now like to argue that Wright does not recognize this alternative way of taking criteria as truth conditions because Wright does not follow Wittgenstein in taking our uses of the truth predicate as relevant to an investigation of what an assertibility condition must be. That is, Wright does not see the ways in which we *use* "is true" as being relevant to the way in which we ought to construe the concept of a truth condition. For, as I will argue, it is only if we refuse to think of the truth condition of a sentence in terms of the way in which we *use* the sentence that we seem to be forced with a choice between defeasible assertibility conditions and realist truth conditions.

To see this, consider Wright's remark that if the defeasibility is waived, criteria will not be interestingly different from (realist) truth conditions. I have argued that this remark betrays a refusal to recognize an interpretation of criteria under which they are not defeasible. And this interpretation presupposes that we think of the truth condition of a statement in terms of the way that the statement is *used*. That is to say, it presupposes that we think of criteria as providing truth conditions for our statements *within particular contexts*. A criterion is a linguistic rule which tells us the grounds upon which we may affirm a statement of a given type. It is a convention which we adopt for a particular purpose. And as we have different purposes for predicating "is true" and "is false" of the various statements that we treat as being true or false, we accept our different kinds of statements as true upon different kinds of grounds. Our various statements belong to different language games.

And we use them to express different kinds of certainty. Thus, on the view that a criterion provides a truth condition of a statement *only within a given context,* an assertion which appears to express a weaker degree of certainty than other assertions that we make is not one whose assertibility condition falls short of being a truth condition. Rather, it is one that belongs to a language game that *admits* of a different kind of certainty. And the *kind* of certainty that a justified assertion expresses depends on the kind of language game to which the assertion belongs (c.f. *P.I.* p. 224). In Wittgenstein's example, the astronomer who calculates an eclipse of the sun does not express the same *kind* of certainty with his assertion that one would express by asserting a statement about the present. But when we take into account the language game which the astronomer is playing and the use to which he is putting his assertion—that is, when we bear in mind the fact that he is making a prediction—we do not take him as being incorrect in affirming the truth of his statement. We understand him to be making a different kind of statement than he would be making by affirming the truth of a present-tense statement. That is, we know what he means by applying the truth predicate to a statement in the future tense. And thus we identify the *grounds* on which the astronomer bases his assertion with the truth condition of the sentence.

Wright does not recognize this alternative way of taking criteria as truth conditions because he does not take our *uses* of "is true" as relevant to the meaning of "is true." And, thus, he does not take the fact that we *use* the truth predicate in different ways as relevant to the way in which we should construe the concept of a truth condition. For on the assumption that the use to which we put an assertion has no bearing on our concept of its truth condition, certain statements will seem to be asserted under conditions which fall short of establishing them as true. Thus, assertions with which we express a different kind of certainty—such as statements about the future and about other people's inner states—will seem to be made on merely defeasible grounds. It will seem as though we cannot learn the meaning of these sentences by learning to recognize their truth conditions. But if we think of the truth conditions of our sentences in terms of the way in which we use them, then the condition under which we assert a sentence cannot be taken as falling short of a condition which establishes it as true. For what makes it *correct* to predicate "is true" of a sentence is a conventional rule which tells us the grounds upon which we may accept a given type of statement as true. It is a convention which tells us what counts as an adequate test of a given type of statement. And the standards of adequacy for the tests of our various statements are internal to the language games to which they belong. As Wittgenstein puts this point, "What counts as an adequate test of a statement belongs to logic. It belongs to the description of the language game" (*O.C.* #82). Or, to put the point another way, what we count as being an adequate test of a statement, and hence as an adequate ground on which to assert it, depends on the way that the statement is used. Thus, Wright's failure to recognize an alternative conception of truth conditions springs from his refusal to take our use of a given statement as relevant to what it means to call a particular statement "true." It springs from a refusal to construe the truth conditions of our statements in a way which takes into account the varying uses to which we put "is true."

Another way of putting this point is that Wright is led to his antirealist project—that of replacing truth conditions with assertibility conditions—because he does not ultimately share Wittgenstein's commitment to the dictum that meaning is use. That is, Wright denies that the assertibility conditions of certain statements amount to truth conditions because he does not take our *uses* of "is true" as relevant to the meaning of "is true." Like Dummett, Wright thinks that language should be capable of systematization by a theory of meaning. We should be able to give an account of assertibility conditions which can be applied across the board, across all the contexts in which we treat sentences as assertible. Or, to put the point another way, we should be able to assign a single meaning to "is true" which is independent of the various contexts in which the predicate is used. And we should be able to construct a theory of meaning for a language which is based on one central concept—be it truth, verifiability, or falsifiability—from which we can derive every feature of the use of a sentence. When we are in the grip of this picture of meaning, the nuances in our uses of "is true" will not appear relevant to the way that we ought to construe the concept of a truth condition.[5] For when we try to construct a systematic theory of meaning, it appears as though there is something outside of language by reference to which we can explain what meaning is. That is, it appears as though there is something independent of our actual use of words in language which bestows meaning on them—and which does so in a uniform way. And if we do not take our use of a sentence as internally related to our conception of its truth condition, it will seem that in predicating "is true" of certain sentences, we are doing so *incorrectly*. For if we hold that "is true" has a fixed meaning, then any given application of the predicate which does not conform to the general model we have given for it will seem to be made on a ground which falls short of being a truth condition. And whenever we apply the truth predicate in an unusual way—that is, whenever we apply it to sentences within a language game which admits of a different kind of certainty from most of the language games in which we use "is true"—this will seem to indicate that the ground on which we are basing an assertion falls short of establishing its truth value decisively. Accordingly, it will seem as though we cannot explain how we learn to use certain sentences, for example, those referring to others' mental states, in terms of our learning to recognize their truth conditions. For we cannot manifest our grasp of the truth condition of "He is in pain" in the same way that we can manifest our grasp of the truth conditions of many other kinds of statements. That is, we cannot directly observe someone else's sensations in the way that we can observe the truth conditions of statements about the outer. And if we hold that the truth conditions of our sentences can be construed without reference to the uses to which we put them, then whenever we put a given sentence to a different kind of use from most of the sentences which we treat as being true or false, it will appear as though we do not understand what would make the sentence in question true. For if we hold that "is true" has one meaning, then the fact that we predicate "is true" of a sentence upon different kinds of grounds from most of our sentences will seem to show that we cannot have learned to use it by learning to recognize its truth condition as obtaining when it obtains. It will seem that we must instead have learned to use it by learning the conditions under which we are justified in asserting it.

Wittgenstein, however, would have denied that we can construe the meaning of "is true" without reference to the way in which we use the predicate. And, more broadly, he would have rejected the thought that language should be capable of systematization. Hence, he would have denied that we can give a uniform account of what it means to treat a sentence as assertible which can be applied across the board, in a uniform way, in all the contexts in which we use "is true." As he argues, the notion that meaning can be explained without reference to anything other than use arises from the fact that "in our discussions, [we] constantly compare language with a calculus proceeding according to exact rules" (*B.B.*, p. 25). And we are inclined to say that the meaning of a word must be fixed and precise in order for it to be intelligible (cf. *P.I.* #79). But we should remember that "in general, we don't use language according to strict rules—it hasn't been taught us that way either" (*B.B.* p. 25). In practice, we do not always use names with a fixed meaning—we may use the name "Moses" without a predetermined sense of which descriptions we are willing to substitute for it. And this does not detract from the usefulness of the name in our language (*P.I.* #79). Similarly, we may say to someone "Stand roughly there," and the inexactness of the expression does not make it unusable (*P.I.* #88). The person we are addressing will know what we mean and what he must do to satisfy the request. Examples such as these should suggest to us that what determinate meaning requires is *not* conformity to a universal standard or model. Rather, it requires an understanding of what is needed by those concerned in a given context.[6] Thus, Wittgenstein would have rejected the thought that the meaning of "is true" can be given apart from a given context in which the predicate is used. What makes it correct to predicate "is true" of a sentence depends on the context in which the predicate is uttered (*O.C.* #205). So the fact that we use "is true" differently in different contexts is directly relevant to how we should construe the concept of a truth condition. It means that we should think of the truth condition of a sentence as that which makes it correct to predicate "is true" of a sentence where this is dependent on the way that a sentence is used. Or, to put the point another way, we should think of a truth condition as a criterion or a conventional way of finding out which we adopt. We should think of it as a conventional rule whose applicability depends on context and which may be modified or revised at any time. And once we have followed Wittgenstein in construing truth conditions in terms of use, we do not have to interpret the fact that we express a different kind of certainty by calling certain statements true in the way that Wright interprets it. That is, we do not have to say that we cannot manifest our grasp of the truth condition of "He is in pain." We do not have to say that we learned when to affirm and deny it by learning to associate it with a ground which falls short of being a truth condition. Instead, we can say that statements about others' mental states belong to a different language game from statements about the external world. And we manifest our grasp of what it means to call pain-ascriptions true by treating them differently from other statements in the context of affirming and denying them. Wright refuses to recognize this interpretation of our linguistic behavior because he does not think of truth conditions in terms of our uses of sentences. But if we follow Wittgenstein in holding that meaning is use, then this is surely the way in which we should think of truth conditions. For if we identify meaning with use, then "is true" has the meaning that *we* have given it. What determines whether it is correct to predicate "is true" of our various sentences are *our* criteria or conventional ways of finding out which tell us how the predicate is to be applied in a given context. And the nuances in the meaning of "is true" are as various as the language games in which we use it. We apply the truth predicate on different kinds of grounds and express different kinds of certainty with it. So any ground on which we accept a statement may be taken as establishing it as true when we take into account its context of use. That is to say: there are no obstacles to identifying criteria with truth conditions once we conceive of truth conditions in terms of use.

We can make the further point that if we think of the way in which we use a sentence as being internally related to our conception of its truth condition, we will not be forced to adopt Wright's skeptical interpretation of the implications of criterial change. That is, we will not have to take the fact that we sometimes change our criteria to mean that we *treat* our criteria as being defeasible grounds. Wright is correct that the notion that we treat criteria as defeasible cannot give content to our practice of making assertions. For it is indeed impossible to see what practical use to which we could put assertions if the convention was that no expectations were licensed. But there is another way in which a community can acknowledge that the world sometimes turns out awkward, that experience sometimes compels us to change our criteria which is consistent with its treating its current criteria as providing truth conditions. What we can say is that a community treats its criteria as being in principle revisable. But there is a significant difference between treating a criterion as being defeasible—that is, as though there is no guarantee of its accuracy—and treating it as being in principle revisable at some future time.[7]

We do in fact treat our criteria as being revisable in the latter sense. For we know that, historically, criteria which were previously accepted have been overturned. And, thus, we can admit as a theoretical possibility that the criteria we currently employ for determining the truth value of our statements may someday no longer be considered adequate tests of their truth value. This is just a point that is familiar from Quine's "Two Dogmas" and Peirce's critical commonsensism: no statement is in principle immune from revision in response to recalcitrant experience (cf. *O.C.* #96, #97, #98). What allows us to inquire— what Wittgenstein calls "the element in which arguments have their life"—is a conceptual system or a "world picture" (*O.C.* #105, #94). It is a system of propositions which we hold true. Some of these propositions are "deeply entrenched" or "hard," while others, which lie close to the periphery of a conceptual system, are "fluid." And if inquiry were to be pursued far enough, we could conceivably revise even the propositions which, in Wittgenstein's terminology, are "hard" rather than "fluid"—that is, our grammatical and hinge propositions.

However, as Peirce, Quine, and Wittgenstein have argued, it does not follow from the fact that no statement is in principle immune from revision that we treat our current methods of testing as being subject to doubt. For, as Wittgenstein remarks, it belongs to the logic of scientific investigations that certain things are *in deed* not doubted. That is to say, the *questions* that we raise and our *doubts* depend on the fact that some propositions are exempt from doubt, as it were, like hinges on which those turn. And if we want the door to turn, the hinges must stay put (*O.C.* #342, #341, #343, Wittgenstein's emphasis). Thus, we cannot accommodate it as a standing possibility that the criteria we currently employ for determining the truth values of our statements may not be adequate tests of them. For a criterion is a standard by reference to which we justify our judgments. And we cannot coherently question whether our standard of truth and falsity is accurate while we are using it as a standard (cf. *O.C.* #205).[8] That is to say, if we did not treat a criterion as being immune from doubt, i.e., if we did not treat it as an objective ground for certainty that a statement is true, we could not use it as a basis for judging the truth value of a statement. Therefore, while we can acknowledge that our criteria are revisable, it is just not the case that we treat them as being defeasible. We treat a criterion as being an adequate ground on which to make an assertion—that is, as being decisive for establishing the truth of a criterially governed claim. And, thus, *pace* Wright, it is just not a part of the convention surrounding our use of criteria that no expectations are licensed by criterially governed assertions. When someone makes an assertion on the basis of a criterion, we *expect* his assertion to be true. We take criteria as determining when it is correct to predicate "is true" of our sentences. And therefore, it is a plausible description of our practice to say that we take criteria as providing the truth conditions of our sentences. The fact that our criteria are revisable only means that it is part of our concept of the use of "is true" that we take ourselves to be applying the truth predicate to what we currently hold as true. And we realize that an application of the truth predicate to a sentence which is currently correct may not be correct at some future time.

Clearly, more would have to be said about how a criterial change can take place. And more would have to be said about the resulting account of truth conditions I have outlined before such an account could be persuasive. I will address these issues in detail in a subsequent chapter. But the important point now is that there *is* a way of taking criteria as assertibility conditions which Wright leaves out of his account. We do not have to think of criteria as being defeasible. And once we have rejected that view, criteria can be seen as providing the basis of a novel conception of truth conditions—a conception which identifies the truth condition of a sentence with a convention according to which it is *correct* to predicate "is true" of the sentence. That is to say, *pace*

Wright, once the defeasibility feature of criteria is waived, criteria will differ significantly from realist truth conditions. To see this difference, let us now examine an attempt made by someone who has been termed a "middle realist"[9] to avoid the problems arising from the "defeasible evidence" view.

## 9. Criteria and Realist Truth Conditions

We saw from Wright's recantation of his earlier position why the view that criteria yield defeasible support poses a threat to the view that they provide truth conditions. If it is possible for the criterion of a claim to be satisfied and for the criterially governed claim to be false, we cannot give content to interpreting criteria as decisively establishing the truth of criterially governed statements. And if we cannot take criteria as decisively establishing the truth of criterially governed statements, then they cannot form the basis of an account of knowledge or an account of what it is to treat a sentence as assertible. The fact is that we do think of knowledge as guaranteeing truth. John McDowell is someone who takes the threat of defeasibility very seriously. Like Wright, McDowell wants to resist the "necessary evidence" view of criteria which says that "criteria are supposed to be a kind of evidence [whose] status as evidence . . . unlike that of symptoms, is supposed to be a matter of 'convention' or 'grammar' . . . but [that] the support that a criterion yields for a claim is defeasible: that is, a state of information in which one is in possession of a criterial warrant for a claim can always be expanded into a state of information in which the claim would not be warranted at all."[1] According to McDowell, the view that criteria yield defeasible support is incoherent because it entails ascribing knowledge to someone on the strength of something which is compatible with the falsity of what is claimed to be known. And such an account of criterial knowledge commits us to the thesis that knowing that someone else is in an inner state can be constituted by being in a position in which, for all one knows, that person might not be in an inner state. As McDowell argues, "since criteria are defeasible, it is tempting to suppose that experiencing the satisfaction of 'criteria' for some claim is to be in a position in which, for all one knows, the claim might not be true . . . someone who experiences the satisfaction of 'criteria' for the ascription of an 'inner' state is thereby in a position in which, for all he knows, that person may not be in that 'inner' state" (1982, pp. 457–58). And this cannot give content to our conception of knowledge as entailing the truth of what is known. As McDowell asks rhetorically, "if that is the best that one can achieve, then how is there room for anything recognizable as knowledge that the person is in an inner state? . . . How can an appeal to 'convention' somehow drive a wedge between accepting that everything one has is compatible with things not being so, on the one hand, and admitting that one does not know that things are so on the other?" (1982, p. 458).

McDowell wants to retain the thought that knowledge entails the truth of what is known by conceiving of criterial knowledge as a confrontation with appearances whose content is or includes the content of the knowledge acquired. According to McDowell, we should think of a case in which a criterion is satisfied as one in which "the appearance which is presented to one is a matter of the *fact itself* being disclosed to the experiencer" (1982, p. 472, my emphasis). For McDowell argues that, unlike the "defeasible evidence view," his own account of what it is for a criterion to be satisfied will allow us to explain knowledge as a match in content between an appearance and a truth-conferring fact. In other words, it will allow us to say that in some cases, the content of appearances is or includes the content of knowledge and that it thus explains our acquisition of the knowledge in question. It allows us to say, for example, that one's experience of rain is the result of the fact that it's raining. Hence, one's knowledge that it is raining is the upshot of the fact that it is raining. That is, it can be the fact or circumstance that p itself that makes us know that p.

According to McDowell, the view that criteria yield defeasible support arises in the following way: there is an idea that what someone says or does constitutes a basis for knowledge of what he feels. This basis is taken as being something knowable in its own right, independent of what it is a basis for. And our correct judgments about other people's inner states are thought to count as knowledge by virtue of standing in an inferential relation to this basis. McDowell thinks that the notion that this basis must yield defeasible support for our knowledge claims is necessitated by the requirement of its being knowable in its own right.[2] For philosophers commonly hold that knowledge must be the result of our having a basis for making judgments, which itself must be taken as the highest common factor of what is available in experience in both deceptive and nondeceptive cases. They note as well that in deceptive cases, our experiential intake is the same as in nondeceptive cases. For example, when someone successfully pretends to be in pain, what is available to our experience is the same as when his pain behavior is the result of his really being in pain. Therefore, it is assumed that because our experiential intake is the same in both deceptive and nondeceptive cases, and because in deceptive cases our experiential intake falls short of the facts in the sense of its being consistent with there being no such fact, our experiential intake in the nondeceptive case must fall short of the facts as well. This leads to the view that the basis on which we make knowledge claims, or the standard by reference to which we justify our judgments, is at best defeasibly connected to their truth or correctness. For example, we may learn to treat the pain behavior that is common both to cases of real pain and pretended pain as our criterion for pain ascriptions. But because pain behavior can also be present in cases of mere pretense, our criterion is taken as being defeasibly connected to our judgments that someone is in pain. It is taken as justifying our judgments rather than as decisively establishing their truth. In other words: it is argued that because cases in which appearances are deceiving are indistinguishable from those in which they are not, we cannot use the distinction between actual and apparent satisfaction of criteria to guide us in making knowledge claims. Therefore, we require a basis for our claims which we can assure ourselves of possessing before we go on to evaluate the credentials of the claims themselves. The only thing that could serve as such a basis is the highest common factor of what is available to experience in both deceptive and nondeceptive cases since this is the only thing which is definitely ascertainable. And because appearances of the "highest common factor" can turn out to be deceiving, criterial support is seen as providing "at best a defeasible ground for knowledge, though one which is available with a certainty that is independent of whatever would put the knowledge in doubt" (1982, p. 471).

McDowell rejects the assumption which he sees as underlying the "defeasible evidence" view of criteria, namely that the basis of a judgment is something on which we have a firmer cognitive purchase than we do on the claim itself. He argues that in spite of the fact that appearances can be deceiving at times, we do not have to picture appearances as mediating or interposing themselves between an experiencing subject and the world. That is, we do not have to think of the objects of experience in general as being mere appearances. We can say instead that in a deceptive case, the object of our experience is a mere appearance. But in a nondeceptive case, what we confront in experience is the fact itself making itself manifest to us. For example, we can say that when someone's pain behavior results from his really being in pain, that person is expressing the fact or circumstance itself. And once we have freed ourselves of the notion of appearances as intervening between the world and an experiencing subject, we do not have to say that our knowledge of how someone feels is the result of our having an independently ascertainable basis for making judgments. Rather, we can evaluate knowledge claims by asking whether, in a particular case, knowledge is really available, that is, whether it is possible in a particular case to tell how things are on the basis of how they look rather than by asking whether we have an independently ascertainable basis for making a judgment. On this interpretation, a case in which someone successfully pretends to be in pain is not a case in which the criteria for a pain ascription are satisfied but defeated. Rather, a case of successful pretense is one in which someone brings it about that the criteria for a pain ascription seem to be satisfied although they are not really satisfied. Or to put the point another way: a case in which someone's pain behavior results from pain is one in which the knowledge of how he or she feels is really available on the basis of the way things look. The case of pretended pain, by contrast, is one in which the relevant knowledge is not available, "although we cannot rule out its seeming to be available." In other words, McDowell's view is that a case in which criteria are satisfied is one in which we can tell on the basis of how things look, whether things really are the way a claim represents them as being. That is, it is one in which knowledge is really available to us on the basis of the way things appear.

What are we to make of McDowell's proposal? As I will argue, his own account of criterial knowledge is one that we should unequivocally reject as being both un-Wittgensteinian and of dubious coherence.[3] On McDowell's interpretation, what it means for a criterion to be satisfied becomes uncomfortably similar to what it means for a realist truth condition to obtain. And by conceiving of a criterion along these lines rather than as a conventional way of testing a statement or an independently ascertainable basis for making judgments, McDowell's view flies in the face of Wittgenstein's thought that "Knowledge is in the end based on acknowledgment" (*O.C.* #378). That is, McDowell commits himself to rejecting the thought that the possibility of knowledge is conceptually dependent on our agreement on what counts as grounds for certainty of our statements or on what counts as being adequate tests of our statements (*O.C.* #270, #271). Or, to put the point another way, McDowell denies that knowledge is conceptually dependent on our agreement on what counts as being an adequate test of a statement (*O.C.* #82). And because he denies that knowledge is dependent on our having normatively accepted grounds for certainty, McDowell leaves himself with no way of giving any account of knowledge. For he cannot provide what is surely an essential element of any epistemology, that is, an explanation of error. This is not to say that we should reject McDowell's arguments that the view that criterial support is defeasible is incoherent. On the contrary, McDowell and Wright are surely correct in their criticisms of that view. But McDowell's conception of criterial knowledge is not the only alternative to the view that criterial support is defeasible. And, contrary to what he argues, the idea that knowledge requires a basis for making knowledge claims which is independently ascertainable or "knowable in their own right" just does not lead naturally and inevitably to the conclusion that this basis must support our claims defeasibly. To see this, let us re-examine the way in which McDowell arrives at this conclusion.

He begins by making the tacit assumption that the only type of "independently ascertainable" basis which we could have for our knowledge claims must be the "highest common factor" of what is available to experience in both deceptive and nondeceptive cases. Because what is available to experience in the deceptive case is a mere appearance which falls short of the facts, the "highest common factor view" yields the conclusion that the basis on which we make judgments is at best defeasibly connected to their truth or correctness. McDowell goes on to make the more general point that the very idea of a basis for knowledge claims being independently ascertainable or "knowable in its own right" necessitates the defeasibility of the relation between such a basis and the claims that it supports.[4] It is worth noting, however, that the more general point does not simply follow from McDowell's criticisms of the highest common factor view. For the "highest common factor" conception of what is given is not the only basis which we could use for making judgments which would be independently ascertainable or knowable in their own right. On the defining criterial view, which Canfield defends, we base our judgments that someone is in pain on the evidence of his pain behavior and the evidence of his truthfulness. A criterion is satisfied—or, in Canfield's terminology, a criterion is *met*—only when the circumstances are appropriate for us to apply our criterial rule. In the case of pain ascriptions, this means that no sufficient number of countervailing statements that would tell against the person's truthfulness can be true. This type of criterial basis for judging someone to be in an inner state would definitely be knowable in its own right. It is independently ascertainable; we use it in evaluating the correctness of our claims. And we could be mistaken in thinking that the criterion for a pain ascription had been met; we could falsely believe that it had been met. But this would not mean that the basis on which we made judgments offered "at best, defeasible support for our knowledge claims." On the contrary, one could consistently hold—as Canfield does hold—that it is not logically possible for the criterion of a pain ascription to be met and for the criterially governed object (pain) to be absent. And despite the fact that we could be wrong in thinking that the criterion of a claim was met, it would be consistent to say that someone was justified or entitled to claim to know something on the basis of his (mistaken) belief that a criterion had been met if his belief that it had been met had been justified. For it is consistent to say that one is correct in claiming to know something on a certain basis even if one turns out to be wrong about what one claims to know if one's basis is correct.[5] Therefore, despite what McDowell's rhetoric suggests, defeasibility is not an essential feature of the concept of a criterion-qua-independently ascertainable test. And thus, it seems that, as P. Robinson has suggested, McDowell's real complaint against criterial knowledge is not that it is defeasible. His real complaint is that it is *conventional.* This is strongly suggested by his remark "How can an appeal to 'convention' . . . drive a wedge between admitting that everything that one has is compatible with things not being so on the one hand and admitting that one does not know that things are so, on the other?" Robinson wonders why McDowell thinks that conventional evidence is less epistemologically serviceable than nonconventional or "symptomatic" evidence.[6] I think the answer to Robinson's question clearly lies in McDowell's commitment to what has been termed "M-realism." For it is most typically the realist who wants to say that our knowledge that p is the upshot of the fact that p rather than the upshot of our having a basis on which we are justified in believing that p. McDowell explicitly denies that his attack on criterial knowledge presupposes a commitment to realism. He writes, "My account of [my] epistemological qualms certainly made implicit play with a notion of truth conditions in my talk of 'circumstance' and 'fact.' But the notion involved nothing more contentious than this: an ascription of an 'inner' state to someone is true just in case that person is in an inner state. That is hardly a distinctively 'realist' thought or one that the later Wittgenstein could credibly be held to have rejected" (1982, p. 461). However, as I would argue, McDowell's thought here is both a realist one and one which the later Wittgenstein rejected. On my view, Wittgenstein's remark "We call something a proposition when *in our language* we apply the calculus of truth functions to it" (*P.I.* #136) is accurately paraphrased as "We call something a proposition—that is, the sort of thing that can be true or false—when *in our language* we have a way of determining its truth value." That is to say, we call something a proposition insofar as we *treat* it as being true or false in our language. And—if we restrict our discussion to contingent propositions, and empirical propositions which is what McDowell is concerned with here—we treat something as being true or false in our language insofar as we have a conventional way of finding out whether it is true (cf. *O.C.* #200). In other words, we do not say "P is true" when we are confronted with a fact which would *make* p true. Rather, we say "P is true" when we recognize that the criterion of p has been met, that is, when we are confronted with something which we recognize as decisively establishing p as true.

In McDowell's view of criterial knowledge, knowledge appears to be something which is just loose in the world.[7] He writes as though knowledge were not a relation between a knowing subject and what is known. And thus he wants to say, for example, that it is our experience of the fact that it is raining which makes it the case that we know that it is raining (1982, p. 474). But surely it is *more* than the fact that it is raining which makes us know that it is raining. For we can ask, does the dog also know that it is raining? Does the chicken know that it is raining? Most people would argue that it does not.[8] Yet the dog and the chicken also experience the same fact that we do. And if we are reluctant to say that the dog and the chicken know that it is raining, then knowledge that p must require something more than confrontation with a *fact* or with that which p is *about.* Knowing that p must require one to have a way of conceptualizing p or a way of articulating p. And we learn to conceptualize and articulate the content of what we know when we learn to speak a language (cf. *P.I.* #384). For in learning a language, we learn various concepts and criteria for their application. This, I take it, is part of the point of Wittgenstein's remark "Knowledge is in the end based on acknowledgment": the possibility of our knowing that it is raining as partly dependent on our agreement on what counts as being constitutive of rain (cf. *P.I.* #354, *O.C.* #114).

I want to stress again that I am not arguing that McDowell is wrong in criticizing the view that criterial support is defeasible. Where I think he goes wrong is in wanting to make the correctness of a knowledge claim depend on something other than what currently justifies us in making it. McDowell wants to make the correctness of a knowledge claim depend on something else such as the way things really are. And therein lies his commitment to realism. For it is this desire which leads him to identify the *satisfaction* of a *criterion* with the truth-conferring fact making itself manifest in experience. But this conception of criteria entails a misdescription of our practice of making knowledge claims. For it is part of the grammar of the statement "I know that p" that it only makes sense to say this when we have an independent way of *finding out* whether p is true. This is precisely why Wittgenstein holds that "I know I am in pain" is nonsense, for there is no way in which one could *find out* that one was in pain. There is no way in which one could pass from a state of not knowing to knowing that one was in pain.[9] And while this example is controversial, my argument does not depend upon it. We can simply say with Hacker that it is *misleading* to say that in perceiving the criteria for A's being in pain, we experience the very circumstance itself. We do not claim to know that p on the basis of the truth-conferring fact itself but on the basis of an *indicator* which functions as a test or a way of telling. A's pain behavior is not the same thing as his actual toothache, just as a man's performance is not the same thing as his actual talent. To see *that* A has a toothache is not to see A's actual toothache nor is it to see *the fact that* he has a toothache. Rather, A's pain behavior is a manifestation or an expression of his toothache. It is part of our ground for judging that he has a toothache, and part of what we will cite as evidence if we are challenged "How do you know that he has a toothache?"[10] By the same token, a man's performance is the basis on which we make a judgment about his talent. Indeed, if a performer is having an off day, we might be led to make a justified but false inference about his talent. On McDowell's view of criterial knowledge there is no way of explaining how this type of error in judgment is possible, and this is why I said that he cannot provide an account of error.

McDowell thinks he can provide an account of error by saying that in successful pretense, one brings it about that the criteria for the ascription of an inner state seem to be satisfied but are not really satisfied.[11] That is, he seeks to provide an account of error by holding that in a deceptive case, knowledge is not really available, but falsely seems to be available. But it is open to us to press the question, what *makes* knowledge *seem* to be available? And it is not at all clear that McDowell can reply to the question. For he does not want to think of criteria as defining features of states of affairs which are ascertainable independently of these states of affairs themselves. He does not want to think of a criterion as a way of telling or as a basis on which to claim to know that some state of affairs obtains. And if he does not want to think of criteria in this way, then we can ask, "In virtue of *which* features of experiential content could knowledge possibly seem to be available?" Or, to put the point in a way in which it becomes irresistible to put it, "What makes it falsely appear that we are justified in claiming to know something?" J. L. Martin puts this point nicely in "A Dialogue on Criteria":

How can you tell that [so and so] is apprehensive? . . . I want to
know what your evidence is. The fact that he appeared to you
to be apprehensive isn't evidence.

—But why cannot the object of immediate awareness be a thing
and yet be our evidence for whatever may be our thoughts
about the material world?

—You have to specify the particular features of your experience
which indicate apprehensiveness rather than, say, restless
anticipation. . . . [if they "look different," then] they "look different" in virtue of particular features which are different. . . .
These features are the criteria you use to tell whether a person
is apprehensive or whatever. . . . They are tests for the application of concepts.[12]

To conceive of criterial knowledge in the way that McDowell does
would be to revise our concept of knowledge as being a relation between a knower and what is known. It would be to deny the thought
that the concept of "knowing something" implies the ability to conceptualize the content of a given knowledge claim. And this ability in turn
depends on our possessing what Martin terms "a test for the application
of a concept." It presupposes our agreement on the features which we
count as being constitutive of particular concepts. Therefore, if we want
to preserve our conception of knowledge as being a relation, that is, if
we want to avoid doing violence to the depth grammar of "knowing,"
we must find a way of resisting the view that criteria are defeasible
which does not deny their epistemological role in our practice of making
knowledge claims. We must find a way to resist saying that criteria are
defeasible which allows us to preserve the Wittgensteinian conception
of a criterion as a basis on which we make judgments. McDowell's
account of criterial knowledge does not offer a suitable alternative.

## 10. Why Criteria Are Not Defeasible

We have seen why the view that criteria are defeasible is a thorn in the
side of the Wittgensteinian who wants to claim that criteria determine
truth conditions. If a criterion can be satisfied even though a criterially
governed claim is false, then criteria cannot be decisive for establishing

the truth of our statements. The classic objection to the defining criterion view, which says that a criterion is decisive for establishing that a given state of affairs obtains, is that it is possible to successfully pretend to be in pain. And it is this worry which causes most criteriologists to deny that criteria are defining: on the one hand, they reason that if "an inner process stands in need of outward criteria," then our criterion for making third-person pain ascriptions must be pain *behavior*.[1] And, on the other hand, they hold that because it is possible for someone to exhibit pain behavior without being in pain (for example, where he is shamming), the fact that our criterion for making pain ascriptions is satisfied does not conclusively establish that someone is in pain. That is, our criteria lend merely defeasible support to the judgments we make about other people's inner states. Therefore, rather than taking criteria as decisive for establishing criterially governed claims as true, these criteriologists take criteria as providing "noninductive evidence" or, as it is sometimes called, "necessary evidence" for our statements.[2] They hold that "if X is a criterion for the truth of a judgment, then the assertion that it is evidence is *necessarily* true rather than contingently true."[3] Or, as C. S. Chihara and J. A. Fodor put it, "If X is a criterion of Y, it is necessarily true that instances of Y accompany instances of X in all *normal* cases . . . the very meaning of Y justifies the claim that one can recognize, see, detect, or determine the applicability of Y on the basis of X in normal situations."[4]

To put the point another way: a criterion is supposed to be what we have *learned to call* evidence, whereas a symptom is what we have *found to be* evidence. The falling barometer (see *P.I.* #345) and the water leaking through the ceiling have been found (inductively) to be signs of concurrent rain, but we have been *taught* to say, "It's raining" when it looks and feels like that outside.[5] Criterial justifications are supposed to have the form "Usually A's are B's; this is an A; therefore, in the absence of contravening data, one is justified in believing that this A is B." And this type of inference is said to differ from an ordinary inductive generalization in that, where a criterial relation is concerned, the major premise is supposed to be *necessarily* true.[6] Criterial relations (or "c-relations") are said to earn this privileged intermediate logical status by playing an essential role in the way certain concepts are formed, and in the way certain words are learned. For example, if the criterial relation (or c-relation) did not hold between pain and pain behavior, that is, if pain behavior did not usually accompany pain, our concept of pain would not be what it is.[7] But because criterial relations are not entailments, criteria are not taken as decisive for establishing the truth of criterially governed statements. Rather, the noninductivist's view is that it is possible for the criterion governing a judgment to be met and for the criterially governed judgment to be false. For example, it is possible for the criterion of "He is in pain" to be met and for the person not to be in pain. Therefore, criteria are taken as "noninductive, nondeductive inference rules which allow us to move from an assertion of criterial evidence to a justified though not necessarily true conclusion of that which it supports."[8] Or, as J. T. Richardson puts this point, a criterion p is noninductive evidence for q if there is a convention that p justifies q.[9] In other words, on the noninductive evidence view, criteria do not provide *truth conditions*. Rather, they merely provide grounds on which we are justified in making assertions.

I will argue that the noninductive evidence view is incoherent. It does not make sense to say that in every case in which we are justified in asserting some statement S on the basis of a criterion C, it is possible to have C and not-S. That is, as Canfield argues, it is not logically possible for a criterion to be met and a criterially governed object to be absent because this would violate a rule of language.[10] If we always had endless doubts about the genuineness of expressions of pain—that is, if we did not recognize anything as decisively establishing that someone was in pain—it would make little sense to say that we had the *concept* of another's being in pain.[11] Since we do have the concept of another's being in pain, criteria must be decisive. It does not make sense to suppose that another person might not be in pain even though the criterion of his being in pain was met. The resistance to saying that criteria are decisive stems from a failure to recognize the fact that criterial rules apply only in particular contexts. The noninductivist is led to hold that our criterion that someone is in pain can be met or satisfied without that person's being in pain because he fails to realize that criteria function as criteria only in the appropriate circumstances. But, as I will argue, once we realize the importance of circumstances to the way that criteria function in our language, the possibility of manifesting pain behavior without being in pain no longer provides a counterexample to the defining criteria view.[12] And, thus, once we take account of the fact that criterial rules are context-dependent, it is open to us to say that criteria are decisive for establishing the truth of our statements.

To see what is wrong with the noninductive evidence view, it is useful to examine how it comes to be adopted. Generally, criteriologists infer that criteria cannot be defining from the fact that criterial relations are not entailments.[13] They realize that someone's manifesting pain behavior does not entail the truth of the proposition "He is in pain." Pain behavior can be present in a situation in which someone is shamming or in which he is acting or in which he has been hypnotized. Nor would it be possible to formulate a list of all the background conditions which would have to obtain which, together, would entail the statement "He is in pain." For there *is* no such list of necessary background conditions which language users consult in making judgments about others' pain.[14] The noninductivist infers that if criterial relations are not entailing, then criteria must be defeasible. He adopts the noninductive evidence view on the grounds that the entailment view is unsatisfactory.[15] As Lycan argues, "It is perfectly possible, in almost any given case that a c-proposition should be true while the other is false no matter how unlikely. So a criterion is not a defining characteristic."[16] Thus, the noninductivist thinks that because we cannot provide a list of conditions which together would entail the truth of some judgment, criteria cannot be decisive for establishing the truth of our judgments.

However, as Malcolm and Canfield argue, it does not follow from the fact that we cannot formulate a list of circumstances which would entail that someone was in pain that we can never know for certain that someone is in pain. There are cases when doubting that someone was in pain would be senseless: "If I see someone writhing in pain with evident cause, I do not think 'Just the same, his feelings are hidden from me'" (*P.I.*, p. 223). That is, there are cases in which we can know, beyond a doubt, that someone is in pain *on the basis of our criterion of being in pain*; the issue is settled beyond question. Therefore, the fact that we cannot provide a list of jointly necessary conditions which would entail the truth of some statement does not mean that criteria are not decisive. What we must keep in mind if we are to see why this is so is that whether we treat some behavior as establishing some state of affairs depends on the context in which the behavior occurs. Conventions and criteria are used—or exist—against a background of circumstances (cf. Z. #492). And, as Canfield argues, we must distinguish between saying

1.  In certain background conditions (things being what they generally are when the piece of language in question is used): it is a rule of language that if C then S

and

2.  It is a rule of language that: if C, and if certain background conditions are such and such, then S.

That is to say, the background conditions within which a convention is employed are not listed in the statement of the convention itself. Rather, the fact that a criterial rule is applicable presupposes that certain background conditions exist.[17] To put the point another way, we can usefully distinguish between saying that a criterion is *manifested* and saying that a criterion is *met.* A criterion is manifested when it is physically present without functioning as a criterion. But on the other hand, a criterion is met only when it is manifested and when the circumstances are appropriate for us to apply a criterial rule.[18] Once we have distinguished between these concepts, we will see how to reply to the objection that criteria are not defining. We will see why the possibility of shamming pain is not a counterexample to the view that criteria are decisive. What we should say is that a case of simulated pain is not a case in which our criterion was *met.* The mistake underlying the noninductivist's objection consists in construing our criterion that someone is in pain as pain behavior *simpliciter.* This leads to the view that in a case of successful pretense, our criterion that "He is in pain" is met but defeated. But in fact, we do not justify our judgments about whether someone is in pain merely on the basis of whether he exhibits pain behavior. We base this type of judgment on several factors, such as whether he shows pain behavior, what we know about his veracity, and whether he is likely to be pretending. Wittgenstein remarks that our criterion for someone's saying something to himself is what he tells us and the rest of his behavior (*P.I.* #344). And by parity of reasoning, our criterion that someone is feeling pain is what he tells us and the rest of his behavior. In order for our criterion that someone is in pain to be met, it is necessary that no sufficient number of statements that would count against his truthfulness can be true. It is necessary that no sufficient number of statements be true that would make us suspect that he is pretending.[19] Of course, it sometimes happens that we do not have enough evidence to determine whether our criterion is met. Sometimes we make judgments which we do not regard as being decisively established. In Canfield's example, we might knock on someone's door to invite him to lunch with us and he may excuse himself, saying that he has a headache. We take him at his word, but later find out that he lied to us. In such a case, we would probably not say that we had decisively established that he was in pain. We would probably not say that our criterion had been met.[20] It can also happen that we make mistaken judgments on the basis of criteria; we can be wrong in thinking that a criterion was met. But in such a case, the latter is what we will say—it will not make sense to say that our criterion that someone is in pain was met but that person was not really in pain. For our criterion for ascribing pain to others tells us what it *means* to say that others are in pain. It is partly constitutive of our concept of pain. Therefore, as

Canfield argues, it is not logically possible for a criterion to be met and for a criterially governed object such as pain to be absent because this would violate a rule of language.

I have argued that the possibility of successfully pretending to be in pain does not provide a counter-example to the view that criteria are decisive. So the noninductivist's objection that pain behavior can be simulated does not pose a problem for the defining criteria view. But it is important to see that, *even taken on its own merits*, the noninductive evidence view is incoherent. For if the noninductivist wants to say that it is possible for the criterion that A is in pain to be met and for A not to be in pain, it is open to us to press the question, "What criterion governs the judgment that our original judgment (that A is in pain) is false?" And the noninductivist has no adequate reply to this question. As Canfield points out, the noninductivist must say one of two things: either the criterion governing the judgment that the original judgment was false is the same criterion or it is a different criterion. If it is the same criterion, then it must yield the same judgment, namely "A is in pain," not "A is not in pain." But, on the other hand, if it is a different criterion, then it does not follow from the fact that A is not in pain judging on the basis of the new criterion that the original judgment "A is in pain," made on the basis of the old criterion, was false. To see why this does not follow, we need only consider that the judgment "A is a grandmaster," made on the basis of one criterion, is not negated by the judgment "A is not a grandmaster," made on the basis of another criterion where the two criteria in question list different requirements for being a grandmaster.[21]

As Canfield argues, what the noninductivist really wants is to get away with having no bottom line, no standard that can be used to settle the truth of judgments once and for all. But at some point, there must be a bottom line. For at some point we do make a judgment, and we do treat something or other as decisive for settling a question. If we always hold open the possibility that our necessary evidence may be overthrown, then the question arises, "What criterion will count as being involved in its overthrow?" If this is something we want to leave to the future, then a crucial part of our claim that p is true is left undetermined. We cannot wait until the future to decide what is to count as showing the truth or falsity of our present assertion that p.[22]

Presumably, what motivates the noninductive evidence view is the fact that mistakes are possible. But, as Canfield has demonstrated, the defining criteria view can handle this fact as well as the opposing view. Of course, judgments can be overthrown. But if a judgment is overthrown, it will be overthrown by the application of the very same criterion that governed the original judgment. If someone makes a judgment that A is in pain and then comes to revise his judgment and concludes that A was not in pain after all, the mistaken person will say that he was *wrong* to think that the criterion was met.[23] And as Canfield and Malcolm argue, the question is not whether we can ever be fooled but whether there is any case in which we know we are not fooled and can establish with certainty and decisively that someone is in pain. Or to put the point another way, the question is not whether mistakes are possible but whether a certain kind of mistake is always possible. This is the kind of mistake where we establish conclusively that the criterion for being in pain is met, but in which it is *conceivable* and in some cases *true* that the person is not in pain (where "pain" is used in accord with that very criterion). On the defining criteria view, such mistakes are never possible, for it is inconceivable—that is, it is a violation of a rule of language—to say that the criterion is met but that the object governed by that very criterion is absent.[24] If we did deem it conceivable for our criterion to be met and for someone not to be in pain, that would mean that we were not using *any* criterion of being in pain. So it would no longer make sense to say that we had the concept of another's being in pain.[25] To see this, let us consider a thought experiment of Hilary Putnam's which is intended to show the possibility of pain in the absence of its normal expression.

Putnam asks us to imagine a race of humanlike creatures on another planet who might be termed "Super-super Spartans."[26] These people *feel* pain and are able to understand talk about pain. They can refer to their own pains and note that they have them. But on the other hand, they have an inbred tendency toward stoicism and an ability to act as though they were free of pain. They would never give the slightest outward sign of being in pain although they could if they wanted to. Thus, this is an alleged example of perfect simulation generalized over an entire race. Putnam argues that if Wittgenstein is right that criteria are defining and that the criterion for "He is in pain" is behavioral, then these creatures are not in pain; but by assumption they are; therefore, one of Wittgenstein's claims is wrong. However, the response we should make to Putnam is to ask, what does it *mean* to say that these creatures are in pain? Judging by *our* criterion, they certainly are not in pain; we would never entertain the possibility that someone chatting happily with friends over drinks might actually be suffering from kidney stones. And if, as Putnam suggests, we say that we know that the Super-super Spartans are in pain because their C-fibers are firing, then we are introducing a different criterion. And if we were to adopt a neurological criterion of pain as opposed to a behavioral criterion, then our concept of other people's pain would be different from what it is now.

And it would not follow from the fact that these creatures are in pain, where "pain" is defined according to the new criterion, that they are in pain where "pain" is being used in the way that we currently use it. What is probably at the root of the hypothesis that the Super-super Spartans are in pain is the notion that "pain" can be defined by inner ostension. It makes sense to say that the Super-super Spartans are in pain only if one thinks that one can say *"This* is what I mean by 'pain,' " pointing to one's inner sensation.[27] But even without defending the private language argument, we can surely say that this type of move is not one that the noninductivist should want to make. For he does think that we employ behavioral criteria in judging that others are in pain. Furthermore, he thinks that our criteria for ascribing pain to others determine what we mean by "pain." In fact, as Canfield points out, the noninductivists link criteria with meaning even more closely than Wittgenstein does.[28] Once we accept that we cannot explain our concept of another's pain without reference to behavioral criteria, we must also acknowledge something else: if we did not treat anything as decisive for establishing that someone was in pain, our practice would not be what it is. There are cases where this is regarded as being conclusively established; where we do not entertain a doubt about it. Therefore, the defining criteria view is the one that we ought to accept. It is incoherent to say that criteria are defeasible or to deny that they are decisive. Criteria do not merely provide grounds upon which we are justified in making assertions. Rather, criteria provide the truth conditions of our statements.

## 11. Criterial Change, Conceptual Change, and Their Implications for the Concept of Truth

We have seen how the Wittgensteinian who wishes to hold that criteria determine truth conditions can overcome one obstacle to this view which springs from the assumption that criteria are defeasible: If we hold that certain circumstances or background conditions must be present before we can speak of a criterion's being *met*, we will not have to interpret a situation in which a phenomenon which we sometimes *treat* as a criterion is present and a criterially governed object is absent as one in which the criterion of a claim has been satisfied, but defeated. We can say instead that in such a case the criterion of the claim was not met. But there is a residual problem for interpreting criteria as truth conditions which arises from the fact that criteria can *change*. That is, there is a problem for the truth-conditional view of criteria which arises from the fact that our criteria are in principle revisable and are acknowledged as being in principle revisable. For we have seen that criteria are a species of grammatical truths. That is, it is true in virtue of a rule of language, convention, or definition that, for example, a man has angina if a certain bacillus is found in his blood. And thus the fact that criterial rules can be revised raises two kinds of objections to the view that criteria provide truth conditions. First of all, it may be assumed, as indeed Malcolm and others have assumed,[1] that if criterial rules are true in virtue of language, then changing the criterion of some term is, *ipso facto*, changing the concept. That is, any change in the criterion of a term will involve a change in its meaning so that when the scientific community changes the criterion of some term they can no longer be said to be investigating the same phenomenon that they were previously investigating. And this opens up a host of worries. First of all, if criterially governed statements are true solely in virtue of rules of language, then criteria will not seem to tell us anything about the world. As Newton Garver argues (in opposition to Malcolm, who holds that a criterion is something which settles a question with certainty), what criteria determine is not the empirical fact of whether or not A, but rather the meaning of A.[2] On this view, criteria may seem to be unlikely candidates for truth conditions for, as Glock remarks, "conventions don't render anything true, but merely establish rules . . . to remove a sentence from the scope of empirical refutation by choosing to use it normatively rather than descriptively is not to create a truth but to adopt a convention."[3] Another worry about whether criteria can be taken as providing truth conditions follows closely on the heels of this one: if criteria cannot be falsified in response to empirical discoveries but merely revised or abandoned, then any change in criteria is going to seem arbitrary. That is, any decision to change a term's criteria will seem like an arbitrary decision to change a convention. Or to put the point another way, it will seem like a completely arbitrary decision to change a term's *meaning*—a decision to which neither empirical discoveries nor principles of rational inquiry can be relevant. And, as Putnam argues, this model of scientific change as being conceptual change does not seem to provide an accurate account of scientific progress or of the growth of knowledge. It does not seem to give content to our sense that, in engaging in scientific investigations, scientists are learning more and more about the same phenomena. Another worry arising from the apparent arbitrariness of criterial change is that it seems to make shifts in meaning or changes in use utterly inexplicable. And by doing so, it makes our agreement appear to be something precarious, without any foundation. The most dramatic expression of this type of worry is voiced by Saul Kripke in his *Wittgenstein on Rules and Private Language* where he writes,

> On Wittgenstein's view, a certain type of traditional and over-whelmingly natural explanation of our shared form of life is excluded. We cannot say that we all respond as we do to '68 + 57' *because* we all grasp addition in the same way. Rather, our license to say of each other that we mean addition by '+' is part of a language game that sustains itself only because of the brute fact that we all generally agree. Nothing about grasping concepts guarantees that it will not break down tomorrow.[4]

Thus, it may be objected that if the truth-conditional view of criteria makes changes in linguistic use inexplicable, it does not offer a very robust account of what communal agreement is based upon—indeed, it may not seem robust enough to warrant an explanation of meaning in terms of actual truth conditions rather than in terms of mere justified assertibility conditions.[5]

The second type of objection to identifying criteria with truth conditions can be put as follows: It may be asked, If criteria *are* treated as providing truth conditions, how could we ever possibly come to change or revise them? That is, assuming that it is true that criteria are in principle revisable and that we acknowledge that they are revisable, what sense can we make of saying that we also treat them as truth conditions? What sense can we make of saying that they *provide* truth conditions of our statements? Doesn't that clash with our conception of both truth values and truth conditions as something stable and determinate?

In the first part of this chapter, I address the first set of worries. I outline one way in which criteria may be taken as being linked up with the world and thus as providing truth conditions of empirical statements rather than mere tautologies. That is, I show how the concept of a criterion may be taken as that of an epistemic test rather than merely as a semantic test.[6] I then go on to show how Wittgenstein's account of criterial change can provide a plausible account of scientific change in terms of scientific progress as well as a plausible explanation of how shifts in linguistic use can occur. In the second part of this chapter, I show how it is possible for us to treat our criteria as providing truth conditions consistently with our treating them as being revisable. I then outline and defend the account of truth that results from these two seemingly incompatible features of our practice.

# I

In *Dreaming*, Norman Malcolm argues that Dement's and Kleitman's attempt to establish a correlation between waking testimony of dreaming and physiological phenomena (rapid eye movements, or REM) rests upon a tacit and illicit change in the meaning of the term "dreaming." According to Malcolm, it is part of our concept of dreaming that a subject's sincere waking testimony decisively establishes whether and what he dreamt. He holds that our concept of dreaming is derived from the descriptions people give of dreams, that is, from the phenomenon that we call "telling a dream." And thus, in our everyday discourse about dreams, what we take as determining beyond question that a person dreamt is that, in sincerity, she or he should tell a dream.[7] In other words, our *criterion* of dreaming is the testimony that a dreamer gives upon waking; this is what we take as settling with certainty the question of whether someone dreamt. Therefore, if someone were to question whether there really are dreams corresponding to people's reports of dreams, it would follow that such a person would have to have another idea of what would settle the question. He or she would not be using *our* criterion—that is, dream reports—as the criterion of dreaming, and, therefore, could not mean what we mean by dreaming. Thus, when William Dement and Nathaniel Kleitman remark that "[the] knowledge [of when dreaming occurs], in the final analysis, always depends on the subjective reports of the dreamer, but becomes relatively objective if such reports can be significantly related to some measurable physiological phenomena,"[8] they are introducing a new criterion of dreaming without realizing what they are doing.[9] For, according to the old criterion of dreaming, it does not make sense to say that a subject could be mistaken about whether she or he had dreamt—that is, that she or he could have a false impression of having dreamt or could falsely believe to have slept a dreamless sleep. But if REM were taken as the phenomenon which decisively settled the question of whether or not a subject had dreamt, then dream reports would become a mere symptom of dreaming, only contingently associated with it; a subject might claim to have slept a dreamless sleep and be held to be mistaken in light of the occurrence of REM. And Malcolm argues that there is no provision in the language game of dreaming according to which the notion of an erroneous dream report can make sense: although Dement and Kleitman take it for granted that the subjective/objective distinction applies to dreams, the fact is that when someone tells a dream or says he has had one, he is not making a subjective report which may or may not agree with the objective fact. Rather, his waking testimony is what *establishes* that he had a dream and what the content of his dream was. That is, 'subjective' and 'objective' are one and the same in the case of dreams, which is to say that the distinction does not apply.[10]

Malcolm thinks that Dement's and Kleitman's introduction of a physiological criterion is an illegitimate move. For adopting such a criterion of dreaming would involve such radical conceptual changes that a new concept would have been created that only remotely resembled the old one. He argues that

> to use the term "dreaming" for the new concept would merely result in confusion which can be avoided by holding fast to waking testimony as the sole criterion of dreaming. . . . Physiological phenomena . . . may be discovered to stand in interesting empirical correlations with dreaming, but the possibility of these discoveries presupposes that these phenomena are *not* used as the criterion of dreaming. The desire to know more about dreaming should not lead scientists into transforming the concept in such a way that their . . . discoveries no longer pertain to *dreaming*.[11]

Putnam disagrees with Malcolm that changing the criterion of a term like "dreaming" amounts to a change in its meaning and in the relevant concept. He argues that Malcolm's radical conventionalism distorts the role of empirical discovery and theoretical construction in the sciences and is thus incompatible with the view that science progresses by learning more and more about the things it investigates.[12] Furthermore, he denies that changes in scientific criteria can be characterized as changes in meaning; he argues that there is no distinction between conceptual change and theoretical change—namely, between cases in which a term is redefined and those in which we discover new facts about the thing denoted by the original concept. As he notes in the following example,

> Two hundred years ago, a chemist might have had only two or three criteria for a substance's being an acid: being soluble in water; sour taste (in water solution); turning litmus paper red. Today we have a theoretical definition in terms of 'proton donor' . . . the theoretical definition has changed and *in that sense* the 'sense' has changed. This is not a case of saying something different because we have *given* words new meanings:

rather, the 'sense' in one sense has changed because we have
new knowledge.[13]

And elsewhere, Putnam employs a similar argument to the effect that
in Newtonian physics, "momentum" was defined as "mass times velocity." It soon turned out, moreover, that momentum is conserved in
elastic collision. But with the discovery of Einstein's Special Theory of
Relativity a problem emerged: if momentum were to remain a conserved quantity, it could not be exactly equal to rest-mass times velocity.
Consequently, it was not only possible but rational for Einstein to revise
the statement that momentum is equal to mass times velocity despite
the fact that this statement was originally a definition. Putnam thinks
that the view that this is a case where scientists decided to change the
meaning of a term cannot be right. For it implies that now we are
talking about a different physical magnitude when in fact "we are still
talking about the same good old momentum—the magnitude that is
conserved in elastic collisions."[14] According to Putnam, our use of a
great many terms is based on the supposition that there is something—
a 'natural kind,' so to speak—for which our criteria are *good* but not
perfect indicators and in the case of such terms, the accepted criteria
are modified in the course of time. He acknowledges that "we could
learn to speak with Malcolm and say that a term is given a series of new
uses." But he thinks that this obscures just what we want to stress,
namely that the changes in our criteria reflect the fact that we are
gaining more and more knowledge about a particular thing.[15]

What are we to say about the debate between Putnam and Malcolm?
First of all, it should be noted that the assumption that criteria are
treated as having a special status in scientific inquiry does not in itself
entail the radically arbitrary conventionalism that Putnam sees it as
entailing. For indeed, as several commentators have pointed out,[16] it is
hard to make sense of scientific discourse without assuming a distinction between criteria and symptoms. To see this, we need only consider
the fact that Dement and Kleitman's attempt to establish REM as an
indicator of dreaming presupposes their treating dream reports as a
criterion of dreaming. For, as Janna Thompson points out, dreaming is
defined, even by Putnam, as a mental event. Thus, if we accept something as an indicator of dreaming, we must have a reason for believing
that it is an indicator of the mental event "dreaming." The association
between a subject's dream reports and the mental event of dreaming
itself is obvious and difficult to call into question. But, on the other
hand, it is perfectly conceivable that physiological phenomena like eye

movements may not be connected at all to the mental event. That they are so connected must be established by means of a correlation with something whose connection with dreaming is beyond question, and the criterion—dream reporting—is in this position. Eye movements, then, are established as indicators in a way very much like the way that symptoms are established. They are indicative of dreaming if and only if there is good reason to believe that under optimum conditions, they are usually associated with dream reports.[17] Nor is the need for criteria unique to this example; rather, as Lars Herzberg and Hans-Johann Glock argue, it appears to be a general requirement of scientific research. For, as Herzberg argues, a distinction between criteria and symptoms is presupposed by the notion of a judgment's being based on evidence. What makes something evidence for a statement p is that it justifies our asserting p. And if a person asserts that p and is challenged as to the character of his evidence, he can do one of two things: he can assert that his evidence was not in need of justification; that this was what p's being the case amounted to. That would be an appeal to criteria. Or else he can claim that he had learned through experience that the evidence he had was a reliable sign of p's being the case. That would be to postpone the appeal to criteria, for nothing could justify our regarding something as a reliable sign of p's being the case apart from its having been found to be correlated with what was already accepted as decisively indicating p. And thus, if we are to avoid an infinite chain of justifications, we must assume that all evidence ultimately derives from evidence which is not itself in need of justification— that is, from criteria. In a language game without shared criteria, there could be no distinction between good and bad evidence nor any procedure for resolving empirical disagreements. It could not be argued that one method of observation was better than another nor could one resolve to take a closer look at the phenomena for there could be no agreement on the meanings of "better" or "closer" here. If we try, then, to describe what scientists are doing without assuming any kind of distinction between conceptual and empirical matters or between criteria and symptoms, their manner of responding to scientific disputes is going to seem arbitrary.[18]

Putnam thinks that he has found a counter-example to this view of scientific discourse in the fact that Einstein revised "momentum is equal to mass times velocity" despite the fact that this statement was originally a definition. According to Putnam, the fact that it was rational for Einstein to revise this statement in light of the Special Theory of Relativity shows that this is not a case where scientists decided to change the meaning of a term: "we are still talking about the same

good old momentum—the magnitude that is preserved in elastic collisions." However, as Glock points out, Putnam's argument trades on the
possibility of oscillating between two different definitions of momentum. What we are still talking about is the same good old momentum
in one of the two senses that the term previously had, namely, "whatever quantity is preserved in elastic collision" while giving up the other
of "mass times velocity." The plausibility of Putnam's story turns on the
fact that before Einstein, both could be equally regarded as constitutive
of the meaning of "momentum." Since the two seemed to coincide
invariably, there was no need to decide which of them should be ac-
corded normative status and which should be regarded as empirical.
This changed when it was discovered that mass times velocity is not
strictly preserved in elastic collision. What Einstein did in response to
this discovery was to accord normative status exclusively to "preserved
in elastic collision." And this amounts to altering the rules for the use
of the term "momentum." Therefore, *pace* Putnam, despite the fact that
the possibility of leaving open the precise status of certain statements
may be a necessary condition for the fruitful development of science,
there is still a distinction between the normative and the factual. There
is still a distinction to be drawn between conceptual and empirical
connections. For once the question of logical status arises, it is possible
to distinguish between those connections which are adopted as norms
of representation and those which are abandoned. The fact that there
may be a fluctuation between normative and descriptive uses and even
an indeterminacy of status does not obliterate the difference between
these roles. To deny this would be to deny that we can distinguish
between the role of an instrument of measurement and the role of an
object to be measured. That is to say: the idea that revisability rules out
a distinction between normative and empirical roles amounts to a fal-
lacy. For the fact that we can deprive certain statements of their normative status does not mean that they never really had this status in advance
of the conceptual change.[19]

We can make the further point, contra Putnam, that even if we
grant that criteria have a special logical status in inquiry—even if we
grant that criterial rules are true in virtue of meaning—we do not have
to say that the criteria we employ are simply arbitrary. That is, even
when we insist that there is a distinction between empirical propositions and grammatical propositions and that criterial rules are of the
latter sort, we still do not have to embrace the radical conventionalism
that Putnam worries about. We still do not have to say that our conventions do not latch on to anything and, therefore, that criterial rules do
not tell us anything about the world. This is a trap which Glock himself

falls into. And it is this view which leads him to precipitously conclude that criterial rules cannot provide truth conditions of our statements. Glock argues that criteria and conventions cannot be identified with truth conditions because "in the sense in which, for example, the fact that the cat is on the mat might be said to render true the statement that the cat is on the mat, conventions cannot be said to render anything true." He holds that to choose to remove a statement from the scope of empirical refutation by using it normatively rather than descriptively is merely to establish a rule. It is not to create a truth, but merely to adopt a norm of representation or an arbitrary convention. His reason for thinking this is that criterial rules, like all statements belonging to the conceptual framework, cannot be falsified but only abandoned. In other words, a criterial rule cannot be revised in response to an empirical discovery or in response to the falsification of an empirical theory. For as Glock argues, the normative status of any type of grammatical rule is constitutive of the meaning of its constituent expressions. Therefore, there can be no such thing as falsifying a criterial rule for that would amount to changing the concept or the meaning of the term in question. For example, we could not empirically disconfirm the statement "All bachelors are unmarried men" by finding a bachelor who was married. For the role of "Bachelors are unmarried men" is not to make a true statement of fact about bachelors but to partially explain the meaning of the term "bachelor." So if we chose to revise this statement we would be choosing to change the meaning of the expression. Or again: if we allow the statement "Jane's three-year-old daughter is an adult" because she has amazing intellectual capacities, we would not have falsified the statement "Nobody under ten can be an adult." For allowing the former statement would amount to a new way of using "adult" and would thus introduce a new concept. Hence, the two statements would not contradict one another because "adult" would mean something different in each of them. Consequently, Glock argues that because criterial rules cannot be contradicted by empirical propositions, the former do not state truth conditions; what is revised when we change a criterion is not a truth about the world but a rule for the use of an expression.[20]

His conclusion about criteria, however, is precipitous. For his argument incorrectly assimilates criterial rules to analytic statements merely because they are both kinds of grammatical rules. Glock's points certainly hold true for his examples "Bachelors are unmarried men" and "Nobody under ten can be an adult." But these are not examples of criterial rules. That is to say: it is true that Glock's examples are examples of grammatical rules or grammatical truths. And it is true that criteria are one kind of grammatical proposition. But not all grammatical propositions are criterial rules. Or, to put the point another way, not all statements of which we predicate "is true"—neither those of the sort "Ravens are black" or "Bachelors are unmarried men" or "Oranges are orange"—are governed by criteria. Rather, as Canfield has pointed out, a criterion is a highly specialized notion. It makes sense to speak of a statement's being governed by a criterion only when it also makes sense to speak of the symptoms of that statement—that is, only where there is a logical difference between a statement of the symptoms of X and the criterion of X. For example, the statement "If something has all the features of an orange (looking and tasting like an orange, coming from an orange tree, and so forth), then it is an orange" is certainly true in virtue of a convention or a rule of language. That is, it is definitely a conventional rather than an empirical truth. But admitting this does not yield the conclusion that there is a criterion for being an orange. For in order for something to have a criterion, it must be possible to distinguish between a phenomenon whose association with the criterially governed object is unquestioned and a phenomenon which experience has shown to be correlated with the criterion.[21] Thus, in Wittgenstein's example, we can speak of a certain bacillus's being the criterion of angina precisely because there is a symptom of angina (having an inflamed throat) which has been found to coincide in some way with the defining criterion. Furthermore—contra Glock—once we realize how specialized the notion of a criterion is, we will be much more reluctant to say that we could never revise a criterion even partly in response to empirical discoveries. For criteria are conventions which we adopt in order to learn more about the world. They are conventions which we adopt in order to learn more about diseases such as angina and other phenomena which are of importance in our lives. And given that criteria are conventions which we employ in order to conduct empirical investigations—and that we want our criteria to be accurate instruments for investigating a world which we don't believe is of our making—we *generally do* revise our criteria in light of empirical discoveries. This point should not be overstated because it is true that criteria are conventions which we ourselves create. It is true that we do not construct a concept wherever we see a similarity but only where the similarity is important to us (Z. #380). And it is true that, as Carol Caraway says, general facts of nature do not completely determine our particular system of concepts (*P.I.*, p. 230). That is, the general facts of nature are not the sole cause of the formation of our concepts; they merely place limits upon our selection of concepts by limiting the forms of life, interests, and types of linguistic training that are possible for

us.[22] But, nevertheless, once we have chosen to adopt a given criterion
in order to investigate a particular phenomenon, then, other things
being equal, we will usually choose to revise our criteria in the light of
factual discoveries. As Wittgenstein remarks,

> Do I want to say, then, that certain facts are favorable to the
> formation of certain concepts; or again unfavorable? And does
> experience teach us that? It is a fact of experience that human
> beings alter their concepts, exchange them for others when
> they learn new facts; when in this way what was formerly impor-
> tant to them becomes unimportant, and vice versa. (Z. #352)

That is to say, given that our interest in adopting a criterion is most
often to conduct an empirical investigation, it usually does serve our
interests to modify our criteria when we discover new facts. The discovery of new facts most often does make certain language games less
important to us and other language games more important. And therefore, unless we have some particular reason for stubbornly retaining
our criteria in the light of empirical discoveries—for example, unless
our use of a particular criterion plays some special role or serves some
purpose in our lives which is better served by our retaining it than our
revising it—we do change our criteria when we discover new facts.
Therefore, despite the fact that criteria have a normative status, it is
incorrect to deny that they provide truth conditions for our statements.
Insofar as criterial rules tell us when we may *predicate* "is true" of our
statements, they do provide truth conditions. For, in Wittgenstein's view,
a statement is not "as such" true or false. Rather, its truth conditions
depend on or are even part of its utterance conditions within a certain
game.[23] Or, as Canfield puts this point, a criterion does provide truth
conditions since it tells us the conditions under which one is justified
in affirming a statement S on the basis of a criterion—that is, the
conditions under which, by convention or definition, it is *true* that
S.[24] Thus, although criteria are conventions, there is an important sense
in which they must be taken as truth conditions: criteria determine
the conditions under which it is correct to predicate "is true" of our
statements.

We can make the further point, in connection with criterial change
and meaning change, that the criterion of a statement is only one
aspect of the use of the statement. Therefore, *pace* Malcolm et al.,[25] it
is not the case that any change in the criterion of a term is *ipso facto* a
change in its meaning, or vice versa. Whether the meaning of a term
changes when our criterion changes should not be seen as a yes/no

issue; it is more accurate to say that when our criterion changes, the meaning of a term changes in just that respect, but not necessarily in other respects.[26] For, as Canfield argues, there are at least four other factors in addition to criteria which are relevant to the meaning of an expression. That is, there are at least four other aspects of use. First of all, there is the fact that our language games are played against the background of certain general facts of nature. There is only a point to playing certain language games in some and not all background conditions, so if the conditions that the rules take for granted change, the rules may well become inapplicable. Second, there is the fact that certain human behaviors such as crying may sometimes be taken as indicative of pain and sometimes as indicative of sadness depending on the circumstances or the external occasions in which they occur (Z. # 492). Finally, there is the *role* that an expression plays in a language game. For example, the role that "He is in pain" plays in our language game is not one of disinterested description. Rather, it is used in order to bring about a certain kind of social response such as sympathy and medical help. Thus, Canfield argues that if there were an alien race who employed our criterion of pain, but who used "He is in pain" *only* as a disinterested description, the word "pain" would not mean the same thing in their language that it does in ours. They would not have our concept of pain.[27] Janna Thompson makes a similar point in her article "About Criteria." She argues that it is not necessarily irrational to resist redefining sensation and emotion terms in the light of developments in neurological research. For "being in pain" is essentially a psychological concept. And we as human beings have a social use for psychological terms such as "pain." Such terms have a function within our social environment within which we have to interact with persons as other persons, make sense of their behavior, and respond appropriately and sometimes sympathetically to what they do and say. So we would be unlikely to change our criterion of pain from a behavioral criterion to a physiological criterion even if we were to discover a correlation between pain and the presence of a neurological state. And, by the same token, given that dreaming is partly a psychological concept, it would not be irrational for us to refuse to change our criterion of dreaming in light of the discovery of a correlation between dream reports and rapid eye movements.[28]

I would like to modify Thompson's point somewhat and argue (with Canfield) that we do not have to change the *meaning* of dreaming just because we have adopted another criterion. For, given that the concept of dreaming plays a social role in our lives in addition to being a subject for research in the sciences, we can come to use the term "dreaming" in two different ways if a physiological criterion appears to be indicated by our empirical research. I believe that this is what has in fact happened in the case of dreaming. In certain contexts, that is, in ordinary discourse about dreaming, we use people's assertions of remembering dreams as the criterion of their having dreamt. When we ask someone "Did you dream last night?" we take whether he or she remembers having dreamt as determining whether he or she did dream. But when we speak about dreaming in a more technical or scientific sense, we assume that the criterion of dreaming is physiological and that someone might have dreamt even if they do not remember it. For as Wittgenstein might say, the two uses of the term "dreaming" belong to different language games. It is probably true that in the case of a conflict, the scientific language game will override the other. If someone appeals to the scientific criterion in arguing that someone may have dreamt even if he does not remember, this will probably be taken as an authoritative move. But for the most part, the language game of science and that of ordinary discourse simply coexist with one another. Wittgenstein describes how this type of thing can happen at Z. #438:

> Nothing is commoner than for the meaning of an expression to oscillate, for a phenomenon to be regarded sometimes as a symptom, sometimes as a criterion of a state of affairs. And mostly in such a case the shift of meaning is not noted. In science it is usual to make phenomena that allow for exact measurement into defining criteria for an expression; and then one is inclined to think that now the proper meaning has been *found.* Innumerable confusions have arisen in this way. There are degrees of pleasure, for example, but it is stupid to speak of a measurement of pleasure. It is true that in certain cases a measurable phenomenon occupies the place of a non-measurable one. Then the word designating this place changes its meaning and the old meaning becomes more or less obsolete. We are soothed by the fact that the one concept is the more exact and do not notice the fact that here in each particular case a different relation between the 'exact' and the 'inexact' concept is in question: it is the old mistake of not testing particular cases.

Some commentators have taken Wittgenstein's point here to be that any change in the criterion of a term is *ipso facto* a change in its meaning and in the relevant concept.[29] A cursory reading of the passage may create this impression because of the phrases "the shift in meaning" and "the word designating this place changes its meaning." However, I do not think that this is the right reading of *Z.* #438. It does not provide a reading of the passage in its entirety and it fails to take account of the qualifying remarks such as "the shift in meaning *is not noted*," "*in certain cases* a measurable phenomenon occupies the place of a nonmeasurable one," and "the old meaning becomes *more or less* obsolete." Rather, I think that the passage should be read in conjunction with *O.C.* #48–49 where Wittgenstein makes a remark, in a similar spirit, about the ultimately pragmatic basis of a decision to regard something as "fixed": "out of a host of calculations certain ones might be designated as reliable once and for all, others as not quite fixed. And now, is this a *logical* distinction? But remember: even when the calculation is something fixed for me, this is only a decision for a practical purpose." I take Wittgenstein's point at *Z.* #438 to be: when scientists take a phenomenon to be the defining criterion of a concept, and when that phenomenon admits of exact measurement into the defining criterion of a term, there is a temptation to think that now the proper meaning has been found. But this is a misleading way of looking at things, for it fails to take account of the fact that what we choose to make a defining criterion is determined by our purpose in using a criterion. What we require in a criterion will depend on the kind of language game in which the criterion is being used. It is not always necessary for a concept that we use to be capable of exact measurement; "there are, for example, degrees of pleasure, but it is stupid to speak of a measurement of pleasure." With certain concepts and in certain areas of discourse, we can choose something for a criterion which does not admit of particularly exact measurement. And this does not detract from the intelligibility of the relevant concepts (any more than the inexactness of "Stand roughly there" detracts from the intelligibility of that order). When we make the "old mistake of not testing particular cases," we forget that the degree of exact measurement that we require for a concept depends on the area of discourse in which the concept is being used.

We see, therefore, that, *pace* Malcolm, we could conceivably change the criterion of a concept without changing the way in which we use the concept or the role that the concept plays in our lives. Conversely, we could conceivably change the use to which we put a given concept without changing its criterion (we could, for example, come to treat "pain" as Canfield's aliens do). And, as Herzberg points out, numerous forms of intermediate conceptual change might be imagined in which some aspects of the use of the concept changed along with part of the criteria. What cannot be imagined, however, is a profound change *both* in criteria and in manner of use *at the same time.* Or rather: such a change, if it were to occur, would be unintelligible. For the aspects of a concept which do not change are what makes the change intelligible; they are, as it were, the hinges on which the concept turns. But in the case of total change, the new concept would have no connection with the old; we could not see the transition from one to the other as a meaningful step to take.[30] Consequently, if such a change really could occur, it would make our agreement seem utterly inexplicable. It would also make our agreement seem utterly precarious for, if such a change were possible, then, as Kripke remarks, nothing about grasping concepts would guarantee that it would not all break down tomorrow. However, this is not the way in which shifts in linguistic use take place. Breakdowns in communication do not just suddenly occur because we do not just suddenly stop interacting with one another. We do not just suddenly abandon each and every language game that we engage in together at the same time. If we abandon some, we continue others, and those that we continue are the hinges on which communication turns, which make changes in meaning intelligible. Therefore, we see that one type of objection to interpreting criteria as truth conditions ought not to prevent us from adopting this view: Wittgenstein's conception of truth conditions in terms of criteria can provide an account of conceptual change which allows us to construe *changes* in science in terms of *progress* in science. In addition, Wittgenstein's conception of truth conditions as criteria can provide a plausible explanation of how changes in meaning can occur.

## II

I have argued that the apparent threat of arbitrary conventionalism should not prevent us from accepting a truth-conditional interpretation of criteria. As I have argued, a closer look at Wittgenstein's account of criterial change shows that it is not in fact vulnerable to the objection that it makes paradigm shifts in science arbitrary and irrational and changes in meaning inexplicable. I would now like to return to the second type of objection to the truth-conditional view of criteria that I raised at the beginning of this chapter, namely, What sense can we make of saying that we treat our criteria as providing truth conditions if we treat them as being open to revision? If criteria are in principle revisable and are acknowledged as being in principle revisable, how could we possibly treat them as providing truth conditions? For if criteria can change, what sense can we make of saying that they determine truth conditions? Is it not a conceptual truism that truth values and therefore truth conditions are stable and determinate? In address-

ing these issues, I will argue that the implication of our treating our
criteria both as truth conditions and as being in principle revisable is
that we need to revise our traditional picture of truth.

According to the view that I will defend here, the sense in which
we treat our criteria as providing truth conditions is simply that they are
the best ways of judging that we have. As Neurath pointed out in his
boat metaphor that we cannot replace each part of a theoretical vessel
at once while we are at sea in inquiry, and as Peirce, Quine, and
Wittgenstein have also argued, we cannot abandon all our ways of judging at once, if we are to continue to judge. And we, as human beings
engaged in inquiry, realize that we have to go on judging. We realize
that our criteria, or our ways of judging, are in principle revisable. That
is, we realize that we may not always take ourselves to be correct in
predicating "is true" of those statements of which we currently think it
is correct to predicate "is true." But while we are using criteria in
inquiry, we cannot do other than take them as providing the conditions
under which it is correct to predicate "is true" of our statements. For
as Wittgenstein argues,

> Now can I prophesy that men will never overthrow the present
> arithmetical propositions, never say that now at last they know
> how the matter stands? Yet would that justify a doubt on our
> part? (*O.C.* #652)

> A judge might even say "That is the truth—so far as a human
> being can know it." But what would this rider achieve? ("be-
> yond all reasonable doubt") (*O.C.* #607)[31]

That is to say, given that in our practice of inquiring, we take our
criteria as determining when it is *correct* to call a statement true, and
given that we realize that our criteria are not immune from revision, it
is a feature of our practice of applying the truth predicate to sentences
that we realize that the correctness of any given application of it may
change. Another way of putting this point is that we *use* the predicate
"is true" as though the correctness of the application of the predicate
were internally related to our current knowledge. We apply it to a
statement only when we can make sense of saying that we know that it
is true (*O.C.* #200). And because, on the one hand, our concept of truth
is internally related to our capacity for knowledge, and, on the other
hand, our epistemic situation is such that our knowledge can never be
considered complete, it is built into our practice of using the predicate
"is true" that the correctness conditions of any given application of the

predicate can change. Is this practice in tension with the truism that truth values and therefore truth conditions are stable and determinate? I would argue that it is not. It is truth *values*, not truth *conditions*, which are stable and determinate. Or rather: to say that truth values are stable and determinate is just to say that it is part of the grammar of the word "true" that it makes no sense to say "The statement 'the earth is flat' *was true* at time *t*." But to point this out is only to express a grammatical feature of the word "true." It is not to call attention to an aspect of the metaphysical nature or essence of truth. (Compare Wittgenstein's remark "Essence is expressed by grammar.") And, as far as truth conditions are concerned, once we grant that our criteria determine the conditions under which it is *correct* to call our statements true, it should be clear why truth conditions cannot be stable and determinate. For I have argued that the notion that meaning is use implies a novel and revisionist conception of a truth condition, where a truth condition is taken to be a conventional rule or a criterion which, by linguistic convention, makes it *correct* to predicate "is true" of a given sentence. If we hold that meaning is use, then what makes it correct to predicate "is true" of a sentence is not that it *is* true, where "true" is taken to mean "corresponds to reality" or "*would be* discovered to be true, if inquiry were to be pursued as far as it could fruitfully go." Rather, what makes it correct to predicate "is true" of a sentence is that we *know* that it is true. And once we have granted this much, then, given what our epistemic situation is, we have no choice but to hold that any warranted application of "is true" must be classified as *correct.* For *we* are the ones who are applying the truth predicate. And, hence, what makes it correct to apply the truth predicate are *our* criteria or our current ways of judging. What makes it correct to apply the truth predicate to sentences are the grounds which we agree are adequate upon which to accept our statements as true. And the grounds which we count as adequate on which to accept our statements as true can only reflect the state of our knowledge at a particular time.

To put the point another way: it is simply part of the human epistemic condition that knowledge must always be considered defeasible. Thus, St. Paul remarked, "What we know now is partial, but when what is perfect comes our knowledge will be complete, as complete as God's knowledge." And we do not think that St. Paul is misusing the word "knowledge" in speaking of "partial knowledge." For given the contrast between our epistemic situation and God's epistemic situation, it is part of the grammar of "knowing" that it can be correct to say "We know" even if *what* we claim to know turns out to be false. As Wittgenstein remarks,

> It would be wrong to say that I can only say 'I know that there is a chair there' when there is a chair there. Of course, it isn't *true* unless there is, but I have a right to say this if I am *sure* there is a chair there even if I am wrong.

> Pretensions are a mortgage which burdens a philosopher's capacity to think. (*O.C.* #549)[32]

It would be pretentious to claim that it is only correct to claim to know something if the statement we claim to know never requires revision. For given what our epistemic situation is, our language game of making knowledge claims cannot be like that. If the God of St. Paul's epistle were to say "I know that p will occur" or "I know that p is permanently indefeasible," his foreknowledge to the contrary having temporarily slipped his mind, he might fairly be accused of being incorrect in saying "I know." But if *we* were to make a justified knowledge claim of a statement which we later discovered to be false, it would be wrong to say that we were incorrect to say "We know." In such a case, we would have to say that we didn't actually know, but only thought we knew. But if our knowledge claim had been justified, it would not be right to say that we were incorrect in saying "We know."

By parity of reasoning, Wittgenstein argues that it is misleading to deny that we are correct in predicating "is true" of a statement on the grounds on which we predicate "is true" of it merely because we may someday have to revise those grounds. As he remarks,

> if everything speaks for an hypothesis and nothing speaks against it—is it then certainly true? One may designate it as such. (*O.C.* #191)

> A judge might . . . say "That is the truth—so far as a human being can know it." But what would this rider achieve? (*O.C.* #607)

Once we have said "That is the truth," there is no point to adding the qualifier, "so far as a human being can know it." What makes it correct to predicate "is true" of a statement is our normative agreement on the grounds on which we are willing to affirm our statements. And the grounds which we count as adequate on which to affirm our statements can only reflect our current epistemic situation. Again, if God were to predicate "is true" of a statement which was going to be falsified in ten years' time, then another being outside the time sequence might say, "It is incorrect for you to predicate 'is true' of that statement." But we are the ones who are applying the truth predicate, and the conditions of our practice of doing so are partly determined by certain general facts of nature—that is, facts about our cognitive limitations and about our being temporally situated at a discrete point in the course of human inquiry. Therefore, we can attach no sense to saying that anything determines the conditions under which it is correct to predicate "is true" of our statements other than the conventions which we employ in our practice.

Does the view that I have been ascribing to Wittgenstein amount to linguistic idealism or relativism? I will argue that it does not, although it might superficially appear to do so. Linguistic idealism is generally taken to be the view that human beings *create* truths with their thought and talk or with their linguistic practices. But it is not being argued here that human agreement *makes* things true or decides what is true or false. Rather: human agreement determines the conditions under which it is correct to predicate "is true" and "is false" of sentences (cf. *P.I.* #241).[33] Some people may still want to call this view "idealism" simply because it denies that truth and assertibility come apart. They will argue that, because it denies that truth and assertibility come apart, the Wittgensteinian view is at odds with the truism that the concept of truth includes the concept of objectivity. It is at odds with the truism that truth is not dependent on what anyone says or thinks, that human agreement does not *decide* what is true and false, and that "people say that p" does not entail "p." For it may seem that if human agreement does *not* decide what is true and false, then what makes it correct to predicate "is true" of a sentence cannot be our normative agreement on what counts as an adequate ground upon which to accept it as true. Rather, what makes it correct to predicate "is true" of a sentence must be something else such as the way things really are or the way the world is. It may be objected that the Wittgensteinian view of what the correctness of an application of the truth predicate consists in cannot give content to the following thought: namely, that what explains why we come to classify some of our prior applications of the truth predicate as *incorrect* are our empirical discoveries. That is, what explains our revision of statements which we previously held true is the brute confrontation of those statements with recalcitrant experience. It is our discovery that those statements which we held as true did not in fact get the world right. And surely that world is not of our making.

But there is a reply to this objection. It is not being argued that the world is of our making. But what explains why we come to revise our criteria and conventions is not the way the world is *simpliciter.* Rather, we revise our criteria and conventions because we have increased our knowledge. So it is not being argued that our applications of "is true" are made correct by a world which is entirely of our making. They are made correct by norms which reflect our current knowledge. And knowledge is partly of our making. It is a relation between facts about ourselves and our cognitive capacities and general facts of nature or the way the world is. And, as the constructivist says of mathematics, it comes into existence as we probe. Thus, the Wittgensteinian wants to say that it is not truth and assertibility which come apart. Rather, it is truth and reality which come apart. They come apart in the sense that although we can have reasons for believing that our current applications of the predicate "is true" are correct according to more rigorous and exacting standards of correctness than our previous ones were, we can never be confident that our current knowledge does not fall short of being the most accurate and comprehensive description possible of that which we are attempting to explain when we conduct empirical investigations. This should not sound like idealism, however, because the world is at least partly causally efficacious in determining what we take as true. And our awareness that our knowledge may fall short of being complete, that is, our awareness that "We say that p" does not entail "p," is reflected in our practice of treating the criteria whereby we predicate "is true" of our statements as being in principle revisable. This is the point of insisting on a sharp dichotomy between the grammar of "is real" and the grammar of "is true."

Nor should this view sound like relativism. For we can make sense of an entire form of life's being shown to be wrong in the light of recalcitrant experience. One form that recalcitrant experience can take is confrontation with another form of life which has an alternative world picture. In such a case, we can say that the criterion for one world picture's being correct in contrast to that of another is that the one can explain all that the other can explain and can also explain things which the explanatory power of the poorer world picture is inadequate to explain (*O.C.* #286, #288).[34] In this case, we can say that one world picture approximates reality more closely than the other. Or to put the point another way, one form of life's applications of the predicate "is true" are correct according to more rigorous and exacting standards than those of the other form of life. That is to say, there *is* a higher court of appeal than the community itself in the question of whether any given form of life is correct. It does not follow from the fact that a form of life is the only framework *within which it makes sense* to say that statements are true or false that any statement held true by that form of life is immune from revision. All that follows is that an entire form of life cannot be called into question at one time from within that form of life. As Laurence Hinman puts this point, "language and the form of life in which it is grounded cannot be said to be either true or false for they must be presupposed as a whole in order for any particular knowledge claims to be judged true or false. Talk about truth and falsity presupposes participation in a language game and in a form of life, yet this in itself is hardly sufficient to shield the form of life from any possible criticism at all."[35] Therefore, whoever believes that the concept of truth is epistemically constrained—whoever believes that there is an *internal relation* between meaning and use, and thus between the concepts of truth and practice—should not balk at accepting the account of truth that I have outlined here in spite of the fact that it is revisionist. For once we have examined the concept of truth that our practice commits us to, the revision which I have called for in our traditional picture of truth should appear to be a justified and a necessary revision. And because the view put forth here avoids idealism and relativism, it does not violate the depth grammar of "is true." It allows us to retain our conception of truth as something objective.

## 12. Why a Revisionist Account of Truth?

I have argued that the Wittgensteinian view of truth should not be rejected merely because it is revisionist. The revision that it calls for in our traditional picture of truth is a necessary and a justified revision: our practice of taking and treating as true the statements which we are currently justified in asserting commits us to denying the thought that what makes it correct to predicate "is true" of a sentence outruns our current knowledge. But the picture of truth as transcending our current knowledge has a powerful grip on our intuitions. Even those who agree that truth cannot transcend our capacity for knowledge may still find it irresistible to say that truth can transcend what we might know here and now. Someone who holds this type of view will typically define truth as the pragmatist does, that is, as what would be believed at the end of inquiry, as what would be believed if inquiry were to be pursued as far as it could fruitfully go, or as what would continue to best fit with evidence and argument.[1] According to this type of view of truth, the predicate "is true" does not get applied to sentences *correctly*, where it is part of speakers' understanding of "is true" that the conditions for the correctness of a given application of the predicate can change.

Rather, the pragmatist holds that the predicate "is true" gets applied *fallibly*. This type of view is articulated and defended in Cheryl Misak's *Truth and the End of Inquiry: A Peircean Account of Truth (T.E.I.)*.

According to the view which Misak attributes to Peirce, the concept of truth is internally related to that of practice or inquiry. For truth is what we aim at in inquiry. The concept of truth that arises from this link between truth and practice is that of what would be believed if inquiry were to be pursued as far as it could fruitfully go. And we, as inquirers, must hope that a consequence of a hypothesis's being true is that, if inquiry relevant to it were to be pursued as far as it could fruitfully go, then at that point, the hypothesis would be believed. Thus, in the Peircean view which Misak defends, truth is connected to human inquiry (it is the best that inquiry could do). But it goes beyond any particular inquiry. Thus, in a way, Misak's view is an attempt to give content to the thought that the concepts of truth and practice are closely connected while leaving most of our basic intuitions about truth intact. Misakian pragmatism is an attempt to reconcile the powerful intuition that most of us have that truth can transcend what we might know here and now with the thought that the concept of truth is internally related to that of inquiry. For apparently, Misak thinks that retaining this degree of transcendence is the only way of giving content to our conception of truth as objective—that is, as not being dependent on what anyone says or thinks.

I will argue that Misak's attempt to square the pragmatist's link between truth and practice with our intuitive picture of truth as transcendent is irreparably flawed. The account of truth that results from the uneasy union of her two incompatible commitments conflates the grammar of "is real" with the grammar of "is true." And in doing so, it radically misdescribes our practice. I will then suggest that once we have rejected the picture of truth as transcending inquiry—that is, once we have committed ourselves to upholding the link between the concept of truth and practice—the Wittgensteinian view is the one that we should accept. We should resist any version of the pragmatist's view according to which truth transcends our current knowledge. That is, we should reject any view—whether Cheryl Misak's, Hilary Putnam's, or Crispin Wright's—which holds that the predicate "is true" gets applied *fallibly* rather than correctly. Instead, we should say that every justified application of the predicate "is true" is *correct* even though it is in principle revisable.

To see how Misak's account of truth conflates the grammar of "is real" with the grammar of "is true," we need to examine the Peircean way of cashing out our conception of truth as objective. According to

Misak, the objectivity of truth boils down to the thought that truth goes beyond what any group of inquirers might happen to believe here and now. A community's believing that a hypothesis is true does not make it true. Rather, what is true is that which *would be* agreed upon if inquiry were to be pursued as far as it could fruitfully go. And there is a parallel notion of objectivity in Peirce's account of what is real: the real is that which is independent of whatever we may think of it. And "the consequence of a thing's being real is that a hypothesis asserting its reality would be, if inquiry relevant to it were to be pursued, perfectly stable and doubt-resistant . . . reality is the 'object' of true beliefs—it is what true beliefs are about" (*T.E.I.*, p. 131). We must remember, however, that it is *only a hope* that the consequence of a belief's being true is that, if inquiry relevant to it were to be pursued, it would be held true. And, therefore, it is also only a hope that the consequence of a thing's being real is that, if a hypothesis asserting its reality were pursued, it would become the object of belief. Furthermore, it is always a possibility that inquiry may *not* be pursued as far as it could fruitfully go. Therefore, the Wittgensteinian wants to say that the grammars of "is real" and "is true" come apart here, for if there are no permanently indefeasible beliefs, there will be nothing that the predicate "is true" could apply to; there will be *nothing that is true*. But on the other hand, all those real things that exist independently of human beliefs will still exist; in the absence of any beliefs it still makes sense to call them "real." They will be as fully real as they would have been if indefeasible beliefs *had* fixed on them. And, therefore, the grammars of "is real" and "is true" come apart; in a situation in which it makes no sense to speak of the existence of what is true, it makes perfect sense to speak of the existence of what is real.

Misak will reply here that even in the absence of any beliefs or statements to which the predicate "is true" could apply, truth would still be "an uninstantiated property." She will argue by analogy that a stone would still be hard even in the absence of any inquirers who could kick it, scratch it, and *find out that it was hard*. And, by parity of reasoning, a potential indefeasible belief which is not actually believed but which *could have been believed* if human creatures had existed—that is, a *potentially believed* indefeasible belief, which Misak would want to call a *truth*— would still be true, even in the absence of thinking creatures who could form the belief, inquire into it, and *find out that it was true*. But it is not clear that Misak's reply to the objection that she conflates the grammar of "is real" with the grammar of "is true" can silence the Wittgensteinian. Indeed, her reply invites an even more serious objection: we can ask, "If, in the absence of any beliefs, truth would be an uninstantiated property, then *what is the force* of saying that truth is a property of *our* beliefs?" For this is what Misak wants to say: she writes, "what would be believed is independent of what is now believed. None the less, truth is a property of *our* beliefs. And truth is what we would find *ourselves* with at the end of a sufficiently resolute inquiry" (*T.E.I.*, p. 132, Misak's emphasis). But if, in the absence of any beliefs to which "is true" could apply, truth would be an uninstantiated property, what can be the point of emphasizing the "our" in "Truth is a property of *our* beliefs"? We can grant that on Misak's view, truth *is* a property of our beliefs. But if, in the absence of beliefs and statements which could *be* true, truth would be an uninstantiated property, in what sense is truth dependent on us, as Misak claims it is (*T.E.I.*, p. 132)? The concept of truth certainly is not being construed here as being internally related to our forming and expressing beliefs, as it surely should be. Indeed, if one were inclined to speculate about the metaphysical nature of truth, then Misak's view, unlike the Wittgensteinian's, would make it easy to do that: one might be tempted to suggest that what actually believed indefeasible beliefs and potentially believed indefeasible beliefs have in common is that they both share in the form "the True." My point here is that the pragmatist's view breaks faith with the thought that the concept of truth *depends upon* and alludes to the linguistic activities of thinking creatures. It breaks faith with the thought that the concept of truth depends upon thinking creatures forming and expressing the beliefs, statements, and assertions which are candidates for truth value. It is committed to denying that the concept of truth is an abstraction from the instances of our uses of "is true."[2] And because of this, it becomes increasingly difficult for the pragmatist to explain the meaning of "true" in terms of our use of "is true." Or, to put the point another way, it becomes difficult for the pragmatist to explain the meaning of "is true" in terms of our agreement on the correct ways of using "is true." And the Wittgensteinian wants to say that when it becomes difficult to explain the meaning of "is true" in terms of use and agreement, it becomes difficult to explain its meaning at all. For if Misak wants to say that the predicate "is true" gets applied fallibly rather than correctly, then she owes us an account of what *would* make it correct to apply the predicate "is true" on any particular occasion. And it is not clear that she can give such an account without invoking a realist conception of meaning—that is, without making the correct use of a word depend on something other than normative agreement. This may seem, on the face of it, like a harmless enough consequence. The realist may say, "Well, fine, I don't mind making the correctness of an application of 'is true' depend on something other than our normative agreement on the correct way of applying it in a particular case. I'm happy to hold that something determines the correctness of our applications of 'is true' *other than* our normative agreement on the conditions under which it is correct to apply it." But, as I will argue, it is far from harmless to snap the link between meaning and agreement this way. For if we hold that what determines the correct use of "is true" is something other than our normative agreement on the correct ways of using "is true," it will be unclear how we learn how to use it. It will be unclear how we could give "is true" the meaning that the pragmatist wants to give it. And it will remain a mystery how we could acquire the relevant concept of truth from our practice. Consequently, if we insist on adopting an account of truth which says that "is true" gets applied fallibly rather than correctly, we will radically misdescribe our practice. To see this, let us turn now to Misak's description of her hypothetical Peircean pragmatist inquirer.

Like any experienced scientist, Misak's inquirer accepts many statements as true, knowing that, in light of the history of science, it's a good bet that much of what she holds true today will someday be overturned. Because she accepts Peirce's critical commonsensism, she does not actively doubt any of the statements which she currently accepts as true. As long as she knows that any given statement which she now holds true was arrived at by a reliable method, her awareness of the possibility that it may someday be falsified does not prevent her from feeling "warranted in accepting it, asserting it, and acting upon it" (*T.E.I.*, p. 124). But because she agrees with Peirce and Misak that the predicate "is true" gets applied fallibly rather than correctly, she thinks of truth in terms of what would be believed if inquiry were to be pursued as far as it could fruitfully go. At least she *hopes* that a consequence of a hypothesis's being true is that, if inquiry were to be pursued as far as it could fruitfully go, it would be agreed upon. It is something like this hope which motivates her to inquire. And now we must ask, *Is this an accurate description of our practice?* What exactly is Misak's inquirer hoping for here? On a Wittgensteinian analysis, there are a number of things she might hope for. She undoubtedly hopes to contribute to the growth of knowledge. She hopes to contribute to the development of beliefs that will be correct according to more and more rigorous and exacting standards of correctness. She hopes to contribute to the development of criteria for judging statements to be true or false which will be the most rigorous, exacting, and accurate criteria humankind could ever attain. But does she hope to contribute to the development of beliefs which will really be true *in contrast to those which she now takes true?* What content could she give to such a hope that would be consistent with her taking and treating the statements she now takes true as true? What role could a hope for beliefs that will *really* be true—in contrast to those she now holds, which she *only thinks are true*—play in her practice of inquiring? The pragmatist's hope here is one that Wittgenstein might well have characterized as "the hope that does no work." That is to say: the goal of alighting on an ultimately indefeasible belief is such that one cannot know *that* one has achieved it *when* one has achieved it. Consequently it is not a goal which can guide us in our practice of inquiring. Certainly, the conception of this goal cannot influence the actions of Misak's inquirer; she can never be said to know whether she is really correct in regarding some scientific hypothesis as settled and whether she may now stop investigating it.³

On a Wittgensteinian view, Misak's inquirer certainly doesn't think that her believing that p makes p the case. That is why she is prepared to revise the grounds upon which she takes it as *correct* to apply the predicate "is true" to p. But she undoubtedly takes herself to be correct in applying the predicate "is true" to statements on the grounds on which she applies it. And if those grounds are overturned, she will say that she *was* correct to apply the truth predicate on those grounds, although it would be incorrect for her to accept statements as true on those overturned grounds now. For that which she takes the correctness of her applications of the truth predicate to consist in is her community's normative agreement on the correct ways of applying the truth predicate to statements. It is her community's agreement on what count as reliable methods for testing their statements and on what count as adequate grounds upon which to accept them as true. And these grounds can only reflect the state of her community's knowledge at a particular time. The pragmatist's view breaks faith with the thought that the correctness of a given application of "is true" depends on normative agreement within a community. For it makes the correctness of an application of "is true" depend on something which transcends the community's current knowledge and which, therefore, can have no influence on its normative agreement nor play any role in its practice of "taking true."

To say that the truth predicate gets applied fallibly rather than correctly puts an unbearable strain on the connection between meaning and use or, to put the point another way, between meaning and agreement. For if our agreement on the conventions and criteria whereby we predicate "is true" of our sentences does not make our applications of the truth predicate correct, it is not clear what would make them correct. Nor could the criteria whereby we accept our statements as true reflect any information, however relevant, if we do not yet have it.

Consequently, and ironically enough, the pragmatist's view of truth also puts an unbearable strain on the connection between the concept of truth and practice. For if what makes an application of the truth predicate correct transcends our current knowledge—that is, if it transcends the criterial grounds whereby we *do* apply the truth predicate in our practice—then it is unclear how we could acquire the relevant concept of truth from our practice. The pragmatist may think that we could acquire this concept by imagining the epistemic perspective of a being further along in the time sequence. She may think that we could acquire the relevant concept of truth by imagining the epistemic perspective of a being who could *see* what permanently indefeasible beliefs would look like. But Dummett is surely right that this type of move does not give content to *our* concept of truth: "If a statement . . . is true, it must be true in virtue of the sort of fact which we have been taught to regard as justifying us in asserting it. It cannot be true in virtue of some quite different sort of fact of which we can have no direct knowledge for then ['is true'] would not have the meaning that *we* have given it."[4]

The pragmatist may think that retaining some degree of transcendence is necessary if we are to give content to our notion of truth as objective, or as independent of what anyone says or thinks. But I have argued that this is not the only way of cashing out the objectivity of truth. We can give content to our notion of truth as being objective simply by saying that it is part of our concept of truth that we recognize that we can be wrong about what we now take true. Therefore, our intuitive urge to construe the meaning of "is true" as being independent of what we currently know is one which we ought to resist. We should revise our picture of the meaning of "is true" as being independent of our current knowledge; this is a use which we should reserve for "is real." Rather, the right way of respecting the truism that our calling a statement true does not make it true, without snapping the link between meaning and agreement, is to say that it is part of our concept of the meaning of "is true" that the conditions for the correctness of the application of the predicate can change. Nothing metaphysical should be added to this conception: truth is what we predicate of statements which meet our current criteria of truth with the full understanding that these criteria may one day stand in need of revision. This is all that we require in an account of truth.

# Notes

## 1. Wittgenstein's Rejection of Realism
## versus Semantic Antirealism

1. The term "language game" has been so widely used that a word of clarification is in order as to what I mean by it and how finely individuated I take language games to be. As I will be using the phrase here, "language game" will refer to any area of discourse which employs methods of investigating and testing that are unique to that discourse. Some examples would include: the language game played by historians, the language game played by social scientists, and the language game played by the scientific community. And I take language games to be individuated in roughly the way that these examples are. Of course, numerous other language games can also be found in more common activities that we engage in. The important point is that the concept of a language game is grounded in human activity: as Wittgenstein says, "the term 'language-*game*' is meant to bring into prominence that the speaking of language is an important activity or a form of life" (*P.I.* #23). Or, as Ronald Bienert puts this point, "the concept of a language game entails the concept of human activities containing language. These particular human activities are fundamental to a particular use of language that is isolated in a particular language game and so are fundamental for that particular language game" (*Wittgenstein's Concept of a Language Game* [Ph.D. diss., University of Toronto, 1996], p. 265).

I would also like to remark here that I will be using the term "language game" primarily as an epistemological concept: in our various language games, we go about testing statements in different ways and we accept our statements as true upon different kinds of grounds. This interpretation of the concept of a language game is supported by remarks such as "What counts as an adequate test of a statement belongs . . . to the description of the language game"(*O.C.* #82) and "The kind of certainty is the kind of language game" (*P.I.*, p. 224). Wittgenstein also uses the term "language game" as a more exclusively semantic concept, i.e., as a way of opposing the *Tractarian* meaning theory. But (with the

117

exception of a few parts of part 2) that is not the sense in which I will use the term here. For a fuller discussion of Wittgenstein's concept of a language game, see Ernst Specht's *The Foundations of Wittgenstein's Late Philosophy* (Manchester: Manchester University, 1969) and Ronald Bienert's unpublished dissertation, *Wittgenstein's Concept of a Language Game.*

2. The reader may recognize the reference to the concept of a rule-following practice as one possible route to the antirealist reading of Wittgenstein. The notion that a rejection of truth conditions in favor of justification conditions is implicit in Wittgenstein's discussion of following a rule was first suggested by Saul Kripke in his *Wittgenstein on Rules and Private Language* (Cambridge, Mass.: Harvard Univ. Press, 1982). Kripke argues that because there can be no fact about an individual nor any fact about the world in virtue of which he could mean addition by "+," there can be no such thing as meaning something by a word. He then suggests the following "skeptical solution" to this skeptical paradox about meaning: according to him, Wittgenstein holds that what allows us to say of any individual that he means addition by "+" is that he uses it in accordance with his community. It is not that the community's agreement makes an answer to a given addition problem obviously correct or that a statement such as "3 + 3 = 6" is *true.* Rather, Wittgenstein is supposed to hold that if this is the answer that everyone gives, no one will feel justified in calling the answer wrong. In other words, Kripke thinks that when Wittgenstein rejected the view in the *Tractatus* that a statement gets its meaning by virtue of its truth condition or by virtue of its correspondence to facts that must obtain if it is true, he proposed a theory of meaning based not on *truth conditions* but on *justification conditions* or *assertibility conditions:* under what circumstances are we allowed to make a given assertion? (Kripke, 1982, p. 74). Since Kripke's initial presentation of this view, a vast literature has sprung up arguing for and against an antirealist reading of Wittgenstein based on rule-following considerations (see especially John McDowell's "Following a Rule" and Crispin Wright's "Rule-following, Objectivity, and the Theory of Meaning," in *Wittgenstein: To Follow a Rule,* ed. Steven H. Hotzman and Christopher M. Leach [New York: Routledge and Kegan Paul, 1981]). I will not be discussing this issue here as it is a different argument for semantic antirealism that I am concerned with. In part 3, I do discuss Kripke's worry that the possibility of a change in a rule-governed practice means that "nothing about grasping concepts guaranteed that it will not all break down tomorrow" (1982, p. 97). For a criticism of Kripke's view, see P. M. S. Hacker and G. Baker's *Skepticism, Rules, and Language* (Oxford: Blackwell, 1984).

3. For a similar discussion of *P.I.* #241, see Jerry Gill's "Wittgenstein's Concept of Truth," *International Philosophical Quarterly* 6 (1966).

4. However, as Lawrence Hinman points out in "Can a Form of Life Be Wrong?" *Philosophy* 58 (1983), it does not follow that one form of life cannot be incorrect in contrast to another. All that follows from the fact that a form of life is the framework within which it is possible to make judgments is that an entire form of life cannot be called into question at one time from within that

form of life. As Hinman argues, language and the form of life in which it is grounded cannot be said to be true or false, for they must be presupposed as a whole in order for particular knowledge claims to be judged true or false. But this alone is hardly sufficient to insulate the form of life from any possible criticism at all.

5. I owe this way of putting the point to Hacker's *Insight and Illusion* (Oxford: Clarendon, 1972), p. 302.

6. I will give a more sustained account of semantic antirealism and of Dummett's argument for it in part 2. I want to stress here that in opposing the view that Wittgenstein rejected a truth-conditional account of meaning, I am not arguing that Wittgenstein held that the general form of an explantion of meaning is a statement of a sentence's truth conditions. In *Language, Sense, and Nonsense* (Oxford: Blackwell, 1984), Baker raises numerous objections to truth-conditional semantics and go on at great length about what truth bearers could not be. These objections do not pose a problem for my view because I am not arguing for a systematic theory of meaning. As will be seen, I take truth conditions to be determined by context-dependent conventions and criteria. And I take truth bearers to be whatever is said to which we apply the predicate "is true"—a modified version of Hans-Johnson Glock's view in "Truth Without People?" *Philosophy* 72 (1997) where he says that "is true" applies to whatever is or could be said.

## 2. The Positive Account of Truth

1. Another way of putting this point would be to say that a criterion is something which settles a question with certainty, as Norman Malcolm remarks in "Wittgenstein's Philosophical Investigations" in *The Philosophy of Mind*, ed. V. C. Chappell (New Jersey: Dover, 1962). The view of criteria that I will defend here is roughly the "defining criteria" view defended by Malcolm and by John V. Canfield in *Wittgenstein: Language and World* (Amherst: University of Massachusetts Press, 1981). I discuss this view in much greater detail in part 3.

2. I am using the term "criterion" in a broader sense than the one in which many commentators use it. For example, Canfield argues, in "Criteria and Method," *Metaphilosophy* 17 (1986), p. 16, that it makes sense to speak of a statement's being governed by a criterion only where there is a logical difference between a statement of the symptoms of X and a statement of the criterion of X. However, Wittgenstein does sometimes use the word "criterion" in contexts in which there is no obvious way of distinguishing between criteria and symptoms, as when he says, "What is the criterion for the sameness of two images?—For me, when it is someone else's image, what he says and does" (*P.I.* #377).

3. I follow Canfield in speaking of a criterion's being met. It is more common in the literature to speak of a criterion's being satisfied. But those who use this terminology generally do not stipulate that the circumstances must be

appropriate for us to apply a criterial rule in order for a criterion to be satisfied. By contrast, Canfield's view is that in order for a criterion to be met, it is not enough that a phenomenon that we sometimes treat as a criterion be physically manifested. Rather, the circumstances also have to be appropriate for us to apply our criterial rule. We shall see that much of the debate over whether criteria can be taken as truth conditions hangs on whether circumstances are taken as being important in formulating a criterial rule.

4. I have taken this example from Petra von Morstein's "Concepts of Forms of Life: Criteria and Perception," in *Wittgenstein, the Vienna Circle, and Critical Rationalism*, ed. H. Berghel et al., p. 152 (Vienna: Hölder-Pichler-Tempsky 1979), p. 152.

5. This remark represents Cheryl Misak's view in *Truth and the End of Inquiry: A Peircean Account of Truth* (Oxford: Clarendon, 1991) where she writes "truth is that feature belonging to all beliefs . . . that would be permanently settled upon on or 'indefeasible' " (p. 168). An implication of Misak's view is that the truth predicate does not get applied correctly. Rather, it gets applied fallibly. I argue against this view in part 3.

6. Donald Davidson, "The Structure and Content of Truth," *Journal of Philosophy* 87 (1990), pp. 279, 300.

7. I owe this way of putting the point to Hans-Johann Glock's "Truth Without People?" pp. 97–98.

8. For the distinction between subjective and objective certainty, see *O.C.* #194, #270, #271. For a good discussion of the distinction, see Carol Caraway's "Is Wittgenstein's View of the Relation Between Certainty and Knowledge Consistent?" in *Philosophical Investigations* (1978).

9. For a similar discussion of *O.C.* #191, see Peter Winch's "True or False?" in *Inquiry* 31 (1986), p. 273. He writes, "the word 'true' is doing no real work at [the] point [where one asks 'But does it agree with reality . . . ?']: it is an idle wheel. And the danger of such an idle wheel distracting us from the real workings of the mechanism are shown in what follows: the temptation to *insist* on the question as though something further were in question, something transcending the boundaries of the language game. Instead of transcending its boundaries, however, we go round and round within it."

10. Glock, "Truth Without People?" p. 96.

11. For a good discussion of our attitudes toward our own practices, see Thomas Morawetz's "Understanding, Disagreement, and Conceptual Change," *Philosophy and Phenomenological Reasearch* 41 (1980), pp. 59–60. Morawetz remarks, "I can admit that I may come to think differently (that my eyes will be 'opened'), but I cannot accommodate this standing possibility ('so far as I can know such a thing') by disclaiming my own certainty. Saying 'I cannot be wrong' or 'That cannot be false' does not have the consequence that I or others will never abandon what is claimed. And this yields a philosophically important general conclusion about our practices: we claim, not wrongly, that some of our beliefs are universal (or universally true) and yet we cannot anticipate whether these beliefs will themselves be given up."

12. Richard Rorty, "Just One More Species Doing its Best," *London Review of Books* 25, no. 7 (1991), p. 3; see also his "Representation, Social Practice, and Truth," *Philosophical Studies* 30 (1988).

13. I thank Peter Apostoli for pointing this out to me.

14. P. M. S. Hacker, *Insight and Illusion: Wittgenstein on Philosophy and the Metaphysics of Experience* (Oxford: Clarendon, 1986), p. 326, rev. ed.

15. Misak, *Truth and the End of Inquiry*, p. 131.

16. Michael Dummett says this in "The Metphysics of Verificationism" in The Philosophy of A. J. Ayer, ed. L. E. Hahn, p. 143 (La Salle: Open Court, 1992).

## 3. Antirealism Revisited

1. The question might be raised here of whether I am speaking of degrees of certainty or degrees of verification. My response would be that statements within different language games admit of different kinds of verification and that this is built into their "grammars," although I am using "verification" in a somewhat broader sense than the one in which it is often used. What I mean is that what counts as "finding out" whether a statement is true varies for statements within different language games. Consequently, the kind of certainty that our conventions and criteria confer on our sentences varies across different language games. It is not that statements within some language games are *less* certain than others, for every convention that we use for predicating "is true" of a statement is treated as establishing it as true. Rather, the difference in the kind of certainty is grammatical or logical. It has to do with what it means to accept a given kind of statement as true. As Wittgenstein remarks, "The kind of certainty is the kind of language game." For example, we can no longer observe the events that statements about the remote past are about. But we employ a convention of treating certain kinds of evidence, such as historical records, as decisively establishing that these events took place. Thus, my account of the meaning and truth value of statements about the remote past comes very close to the one given by Cheryl Misak in *Truth and the End of Inquiry*, p. 137. She writes, "we must be careful not to conflate unverifiability and undecidability." To decide or agree that something is the case is not the same as to verify by direct observation that it is the case. For the reasons for deciding on something might have little to do with sensory evidence. . . . Statements about the past . . . can, in principle, be candidates for the truth predicate despite the fact that they have no direct link with empirical observation. [For] example, although we have not seen Napoleon Bonaparte, we cannot explain the documents and monuments referring to him without supposing that he existed."

2. See Canfield, *Wittgenstein: Language and World*, p. 117.

3. I thank Cheryl Misak for urging me to take this seriously as a possible counter-example.

4. In other words, just as we learn the concept "pain" when we learn language, we acquire the concept "red" when we learn the use of the word "red." It is not being argued that the word "red" means "what we agree to call "red," but rather that if the word "red" is taken to refer to a private sensation rather than to the color samples which we call "red," there is no way of explaining the public linguistic use of the word "red."

## Part II. From "Meaning is Use" to Semantic Antirealism

1. Dummett shows some ambivalence on this point. In some places he writes as though he wants to *identify* truth conditions with assertibility conditions. For example, in "Realism," he says "[For the antirealist], understanding a statement consists in knowing what counts as evidence adequate for the assertion of the statement, and the truth of the statement can consist only in the existence of such evidence" (*Truth and Other Enigmas* [Cambridge, Mass.: Harvard University Press, 1978], p. 155). However, in other places he writes as though he definitely wants to replace truth conditions with assertibility conditions. In the preface to *Truth and Other Enigmas,* he says "it is essential to the concept of pain both that we judge on the basis of behavior and that such judgments are frequently defeasible" (p. xxxviii). Thus, he concludes that "[t]he account of meaning in terms of truth conditions has to be replaced by one in terms of the conditions under which we are justified in making statements [such as "Jones is in pain"], including ones where the justification may be overturned." (p. xxxvii). What follows hinges on Dummett's speaking in the second way. As Richard Kirkham rightly points out, all of Dummett's arguments on the question directly support the second reading ("What Dummett Says About Truth and Linguistic Competence," *Mind* 98 [1989], p. 210).

## 4. The Acquisition Argument and the Manifestation Criterion

1. See "What Is a Theory of Meaning I," in *Mind and Language: The Wolfson College Lectures,* ed. S. Guttenplan (Oxford: Clarendon, 1975) and "What Is a Theory of Meaning II," in *Truth and Meaning,* ed. G. Evans and J. McDowell (Oxford: 1976).

2. This remark represents Kirkham's explication of the concept of "implicit knowledge" (1989, pp. 211–15). According to Kirkham, implicit knowledge, for Dummett, means nonpropositional knowledge. Knowing a language is supposed to be a knowing-how, not a knowing-that. That is, it is ability knowledge, not propositional knowledge. But the practical ability that a competent speaker has can be represented by propositions, that is, by axioms and theorems of a theory of meaning, including those which specify the references of terms and the application of predicates. And it is these axioms and theorems

which model what a speaker knows when he knows a language. He does not *really* know them, but it is *as if* he knows them. As Kirkham illustrates this point, touch-typing ability does not presuppose algorithmic knowledge of the relative positions of the keys, but it could be represented that way. And then if a nontypist were to memorize those algorithms and could make fast enough inferences, he would also be able to touch-type. In the same way, if someone who was not competent in a given language were to memorize the propositions of a theory of meaning for that language, then, if he could make fast enough inferences, his linguistic ability would match the native speaker's. I find Kirkham's explication of "implicit knowledge" perspicuous. However, it is problematic to read Dummett this way because Dummett also writes as though "implicit knowledge" must be taken as referring to actual sentences which a speaker would first acquire *from which* he could infer the propositions of a theory of meaning for that language (and nothing else). I prefer the second reading. I agree with Kirkham that what a competent speaker knows is not the propositions of a theory of meaning for a language. But I think "implicit knowledge" must still be taken as knowledge of actual sentences. For whereas implicit knowledge must be manifested *by* a practical ability, it is still knowledge *of* meaning and thus is not merely a knowing-how such as touch-typing or riding a bicycle.

3. I owe this way of putting the point to Dag Prawitz's "Dummett on a Theory of Meaning and Its Impact on Logic," in *Michael Dummett: Contributions to Philosophy*, ed. Barry M. Taylor, (Dordrecht: Martinus Nijhoff, 1987), p. 123.

## 5. Antirealism Presupposes Realism

1. Some commentators have objected to Dummett's way of presenting the case for *rejecting realism* in terms of a case for *rejecting bivalence*. As Loar and Rosen have pointed out, Dummett tends to write as though a commitment to bivalence were a necessary condition of realism (Brian Loar, "Truth Beyond All Verificationism," in *Michael Dummett: Contribution to Philosophy*, p. 86; Gideon Rosen, "The Shoals of Language," *Mind* 104 [1995]). But, as Rosen argues, one could be a realist and still hold that bivalence fails for statements containing vague predicates such as "Jones is bald" said of a man with a dozen scattered hairs. That is, one could accept truth value gaps due to vagueness and still hold that *facts* about baldness and the rest obtain independently of our minds and our linguistic practices. I will not address this issue here. For a discussion of it, see Rosen's "The Shoals of Language," pp. 6–7.

2. For example, at the beginning of *Frege's Conception of Numbers as Objects* (Aberdeen: Aberdeen University Press, 1983, p. xv), Crispin Wright asks, is it not "natural to say that Goldbach's Conjecture must be determinately either true or false?"

3. This raises the question, "What will we say about Goldbach's Conjecture if it is proved?" The answer to this, as Stuart Shanker argues, is that a mathematical proposition is internally related to its proof. So when a proposition

has been created by the construction of a proof, what we have is a new proposition and not the conjecture in a different garb (see Stuart Shanker, *Wittgenstein and the Turning Point in Philosophy of Mathematics,* [Albany: State University of New York Press, 1987], p. 58). As Wittgenstein puts this point, "A proposition construed in such a way that it could be undetectably true is completely detached from reality and no longer functions as a proposition" (*P.R.* #225).

4. See Shanker's *Wittgenstein and the Turning Point,* pp. 64, 57.

5. Janna Thompson makes a similar point in "About Criteria," *Ratio* 13 (1971), pp. 37–39. As Thompson argues, "being in pain" is essentially a psychological concept. And we as human beings have a social use for psychological terms such as "pain." That is, such terms have a function within our social environment within which we have to interact as persons with other persons, make sense of their actions, and respond appropriately and sometimes sympathetically to what they say and do. So we would be unlikely to change our criterion of pain from a behavioral criterion to a physiological criterion even if we were to discover a correlation between pain and the presence of a neurological state.

6. It might be objected that if statements about the remote past do not express the same type of certainty as statements about the present, there is then no reason to resist the temptation to call our uses of the former statements mere warranted assertion—or as a lower-class kind of truth. The right reply to this is that our uses of all statements can be called "warranted assertion" in this sense. That is, in every language game or area of discourse, we have grounds on which we assert any given statement, grounds which are relevant to the way in which we use the statement and which are germane to the language game to which the statement belongs. It is just that different language games admit of different degrees of certainty. And it is not clear why our uses of statements about the remote past ought to be called "a lower-class kind of truth." It is simply an instance of the truth predicate being applied on a different kind of ground—not on a "lower" kind of ground.

7. I am not arguing here that statements about the remote past are governed by criteria. I do not think that we have ways of actually testing these statements. But we can certainly make the point that we learn when to call these statements "true" by learning on what basis we are to count them as true. The existence of a legend is such a basis. That is, the existence of a legend surrounding a historical figure is our evidence that such a person did once live. We have a convention of treating as valid the inference that since many things have long been *said* of Moses and Christ and William Tell, these persons did actually live in the remote past. Furthermore, historians employ methods, unique to their discipline, of distinguishing legends from mere fictional stories.

8. Notice that, for this reason, Wittgenstein's account of our grasp of the truth conditions of past-tense statements is not vulnerable to the antirealist objection which can be leveled at John McDowell's account in "On 'The Reality of the Past' " (in *Action and Interpretation: Studies in the Philosophy of the Social Sciences,* ed. Christopher Hookway and Philip Petit [Cambridge, England: Cambridge Univ. Press, 1978]). McDowell holds that the realist can meet the

antirealist's challenge to manifest his grasp of past-tense statements' truth conditions without appealing to the truth value link. He argues that knowledge of the past occurrence of an event is *sometimes* noninferential; events make impacts on our senses when they occur and leave persistent traces on our nervous systems afterward. And we attain competence in past-tense statements of the problematic sort by thus acquiring a conception of the *kind* of circumstances that would constitute their truth conditions. Hence, the realist need not accept the antirealist's view that the circumstances justifying assertions must belong to the sort which are available to awareness *whenever* they obtain. He can hold instead that they can be of the sort which are *sometimes* available to consciousness—as on occasions which constitute opportunities for training— and at other times not. For what we are dealing with is a *general* competence with statements about the past. And the ascription of a subcompetence with past-tense statements whose truth conditions are unmanifestable is justified since "the *general* competence of which it is an application can be observed in the operations of others of its applications. The antirealist will surely reply here, however, that competence with past-tense statements of the problematic sort is just *not an application* of the general competence with statements about the past. For McDowell's account of how we acquire training in the circumstances which justify the assertions of past-tense statements leaves statements about the *remote* past quite out of the picture. The virtue of Wittgenstein's account of our grasp of statements about the remote past is that it treats them as belonging to a different language game from statements about the recent past. So the antirealist can no longer claim that no account has been given of our grasp of statements about the remote past except on the (dis)analogous model of statements about the recent past—nor, therefore, that no *adequate* account has been given.

## 6. Tensions between Wittgenstein and Dummett

1. See Akeel Bilgrami's "Meaning, Holism, and Use," in *Truth and Interpretation: Perspectives on the Philosophy of Donald Davidson*, ed. Ernest LePore (New York: Blackwell, 1986) and Simon Blackburn's "Manifesting Realism" in *Midwest Studies in Philosophy* 14 (1989). Bilgrami argues that a scientific realist could claim to manifest his grasp of the truth conditions of a theoretical sentence of a scientific theory by his use of it in successful explanations. He would accordingly decline to answer the question of whether he could recognize these truth conditions as obtaining on the grounds that this is irrelevant to the adequacy of his reply to the question of how he manifests his understanding. And Dummett has no ground for challenging the adequacy of the realist's manifestation without appealing to his antiholist commitments.

2. I have taken this example from Kirkham's "What Dummett Says About Truth and Linguistic Competence," *Mind* 98 (1989), p. 219.

3. Blackburn notices that construing our grasp of truth conditions in terms of sensitivity to evidential pressure will make grasping a truth condition

appear very similar to grasping an assertibility condition. He denies, however, that this is a "victory for the antirealist." For, as he argues, "A friend of truth conditions . . . will protest that he never wanted a grasp of them to play an explanatory role . . . in an account of understanding. He may have been content with an equation between understanding and grasp of truth-conditions each to be equally explained . . . by identifying the capacities that count as the exercise of understanding" (p. 36). But Blackburn's reply here is inadequate because the account of truth he is committed to does allow for the possibility of transcendence (cf. p. 41) even while he wants to explain our *understanding* of truth conditions in terms of neighboring abilities. And this leaves him open to just the objection that Dummett wants to make: that no content has been given to the equation between understanding and grasp of truth conditions. For example, Blackburn remarks (p. 41) that construing the truth of p realistically need not mean construing it in such a way that we could never tell whether we were nearer or farther from it since the realist wants to say that there are better and worse reasons for believing that p. But if the truth of p is possibly transcendent, there can no longer be any necessary connection between having good reasons for believing it and being justified in inferring from this that we are nearer to its truth. So Dummett can say that if truth conditions are not to play an explanatory role in an account of understanding, then his objection holds: a (realist) truth-conditional theory of meaning cannot give content to what a speaker's understanding consists in. For Blackburn's account severs the link between our grasp of actual truth conditions and our grasp of assertibility conditions: his explanation of what counts as grasping a truth condition makes it an account of grasping something quite different. Thus, Blackburn has not offered a convincing defense of a (realist) truth-conditional theory of meaning. Instead, he has given a convincing argument for identifying truth conditions with assertibility conditions.

4. See Dummett, *Frege: Philosophy of Language* (London: Duckworth, 1973) p. 59.

5. *Frege: Philosophy of Language*, p. 681.

6. See John V. Canfield "Wittgenstein versus Quine: The Passage into Language," in *Wittgenstein and Quine*, ed. Hans Johann Glock and Robert L. Arrington (London: Routledge, 1996), p. 26.

7. I owe the preceding discussion of the holistic nature of semantic content and the inferential nature of concepts to Robert Brandom's *Making It Explicit* (Cambridge, Mass.: Harvard University Press, 1994), pp. 89–91.

8. For an empirical study which bears out this hypothesis about language learning, see John Canfield's "The Living Language: Wittgenstein and the Empirical Study of Communication," *Language Sciences* 15 (1993). Canfield's findings suggest that the child's first utterances are utterances which are embedded in language games or customs which the child has acquired. That is, its first utterances can be described as "moves within language games." Canfield argues that the child at some point does pass spontaneously into language—but on the basis of mastery of an antecedent pattern of interaction, such as making natural gestures and thereby being given something.

9. See Bilgrami, "Meaning, Holism, and Use," p. 117.

10. See F. Waismann, *The Principles of Linguistic Philosophy* (London: Macmillan, 1965) pp. 111–12.

11. For an account of the transition from language acquisition to language mastery which focuses on the developmental process, see John McDowell's "Antirealism and the Epistemology of Understanding," in *Meaning and Understanding,* ed. Herman Parret and Jacques Bouveresse (Berlin: Wade Gruyter, 1991), pp. 239–41. McDowell argues that learning a language "makes a new range of facts available to our awareness, not previously within our perceptual ken—facts about what people are saying. For light to dawn is for one's dealings with language to cease to be blind responses to stimuli: it is to come to hear utterances as expressive of thoughts and to make one's own utterances expressive of thoughts. It is to come to have something to say and to conceive of others as having something to say as opposed to merely making and reacting to sounds in a way that one has been drilled to feel comfortable with. And light does not dawn piecemeal over particular sentences; light gradually dawns over the whole of a more or less coherent totality of sentences that we have been drilled into accepting. Thus, working one's way into language is working one's way into a conception of the world, including a conception of oneself as a person among others.

12. See Stuart Shanker's "The Conflict Between Wittgenstein and Quine on the Nature of Language and Cognition and Its Implications for Constraint Theory," in *Wittgenstein and Quine,* p. 235 ed. Hans-Johann Glock and Robert L. Arrington (London: Routledge, 1996).

13. I owe the preceding discussion to Stuart Shanker's "The Conflict Between Wittgenstein and Quine on the Nature of Language and Cognition and Its Inplications for Constraint Theory," pp. 233–37.

14. Indeed, as Simon Blackburn points out (1989, p. 34), Dummett himself relies on "neighboring abilities" to explain our grasp of assertibility conditions. Otherwise he could not allow the intelligibility of undecidable sentences. And, as Neil Tenant points out (1987, p. 44), Dummett's molecularism is not consistent; he makes conflicting remarks about whether we can grasp a sentence's content without knowing others. He says (*T.O.E.*, p. 304) that a sentence must be taken as saying something on its own, but he also says that "a grasp of the meaning of any sentence must, even on a molecular view of language, depend on mastery of some fragment of the language which may, in some cases, be quite extensive" (*T.O.E.*, p. 304). As Tenant remarks, "if understanding requires fragments, our understanding of the demands of molecularism fragments."

15. See McDowell, "Antirealism and the Epistemology of Understanding," p. 237.

16. For example, Frege denied (in "The Thought: A Logical Inquiry," in *Philosophical Logic,* ed. P. F. Strawson [Oxford: Oxford University Press, 1964]) that meaning can be private without holding that meaning is essentially intersubjective: he construed the objectivity of sense by postulating mind-

independent thoughts existing in a third realm which are graspable by all speakers without making the *shareability* of thoughts their primary feature.

17. For an account of how the attempt to account for the objectivity of meaning without reference to its intersubjectivity leads to a doctrine of privacy for certain parts of language, see my "On the Link between Frege's Platonic-Realist Semantics and his Doctrine of Private Senses," in *Philosophy* 72 (1997).

18. See V. W. O. Quine, *The Pursuit of Truth* (Cambridge, Mass.: Harvard University Press, 1990), p. 94.

19. V. W. O. Quine, "Two Dogmas of Empiricism," in *From a Logical Point of View* (Cambridge, Mass.: Harvard University Press, 1953), p. 41.

20. The clarification given here is taken from Kenneth Winkler's "Skepticism and Antirealism," *Mind* 94 (1995), p. 45.

21. "The Metaphysics of Verificationism" in *The Philosophy of A. J. Ayer*, ed. Hahn, p. 133.

22. See Winkler, "Skepticism and Antirealism," (1995), p. 46.

23. For a good discussion of the tension between Dummett's revisionism and his employment of "meaning is use," see Crispin Wright's "Dummett and Revisionism" in *Michael Dummett: Contributions to Philosophy*, ed. Taylor (Dordrecht: Martinus Nijhoff, 1987). As Wright argues, the concept of objectivity which Dummett needs to justify his revisionism requires that it is "fixed, determinate, and in no sense conditional on our ratification what use in a new context of an expression accords with our previous use of it" (p. 36). And it is far from obvious how this can be explained without reinvoking the notion of transcendent objectivity which the antirealist repudiates. Thus, Dummett has essayed to occupy an incoherent middle position between Frege and the later Wittgenstein because his explanation of why antirealism should be revisionist at all requires an appeal to the objectivity of meaning to which his antirealist entitlement needs making out.

## 7. Semantic Antirealism Is Inconsistent

1. For another discussion of the tension between Principle C and Principle K, see Goran Sundholm's "Vestiges of Realism," in *The Philosophy of Michael Dummett*, ed. Brian McGuinness (The Netherlands: Kluwer Academic Publishers, 1994), pp. 139–40.

## Part III. Why a Revisionist Account of Truth?

1. Judith Genova reads Wittgenstein as proposing a radical revision in our concept of knowledge as guaranteeing truth. According to her, "the most radical implication of Wittgenstein's challenge to Descartes is his questioning of the long-standing belief that I know that p implies p or the truth of the proposition in question" (*Wittgenstein: A Way of Seeing* [New York: Routledge, 1995], p. 189).

This cannot be right. I will later argue that the passage on which she bases this interpretation should be read in a different way.

## 8. Criteria and Justification Conditions

1. See his "Antirealist Semantics: The Role of Criteria," in *Realism, Meaning, and Truth* (Oxford: Blackwell, 1987).

2. What Wright actually says is that criteria will not be interestingly different from public truth conditions if defeasibility is waived. However, it is clear from his remarks that he is thinking of truth conditions as realist truth conditions. For Wright, what distinguishes criteria and assertibility conditions from truth conditions is that they *fall short* of being truth conditions—that is, they're not decisive for establishing the truth of what is asserted. And nowhere in "Second Thoughts About Criteria" does he suggest that we should *identify* truth with assertibility.

3. Wright mentions a fifth feature of criteria, that the criteria of a statement will typically be multiple. This feature plays no role in his argument so I leave it out of my discussion. But I follow Wright in this section in speaking of criteria in the plural.

4. Later in this chapter, I will call into question whether we can make sense of such a distinction without snapping the link between justification and practice. And the picture of correct assertion or justification as being possibly recognition-transcendent—and hence unconnected to a practice—is one that Wright himself is anxious to avoid.

5. This is why a conception of meaning in terms of use must undermine the notion, so popular in contemporary philosophy of language, that language ought to be capable of systematization by a theory of meaning. For an argument that there is no such thing as a theory of meaning for a language, and therefore no such thing as a significant contribution to such an enterprise, see Baker's *Language, Sense, and Nonsense*. See also his *Skepticism, Rules, and Language*.

6. I owe this way of putting the point to Oswald Hanfling's *Wittgenstein's Later Philosophy* (Albany: State University of New York Press, 1989).

7. John McDowell makes a similar point in "Criteria, Defeasibility, and Knowledge," *Proceedings of the British Academy* 68 (1982), p. 461. He writes, "We are told to model our conception of 'antirealist' semantics on the mathematical intuitionists' explanation of logical constants in terms of proof conditions. But proof is precisely not defeasible, so there is nothing in the model to make us comfortable with the defeasibility of criteria. . . . Wittgenstein, On Certainty, #651— cited by Wright at page 244 of 'Antirealist Semantics: the role of criteria' makes a point about *fallibility*. Reliance on a *defeasible* basis is quite another matter."

8. Of course, we can question whether a criterion is an adequate way of judging. In this situation, there will be a fluctuation between criteria and symptoms. But if we do this, we will be employing a new way of judging. We will not be questioning whether a certain method of testing is adequate according to the old standards of adequacy.

9. McDowell first applies this term to himself in "On 'The Reality of the Past' " where he argues that "M-realism" is not vulnerable to the antirealist objections which can be made against truth value link realism. In "Realism, Truth Value Links, Other Minds, and the Past," *Ration* 22 (1980), Crispin Wright argues that M-realism fares no better than truth value link realism.

## 9. Criteria and Realist Truth Conditions

1. "Criteria, Defeasibility, and Knowledge," in *Proceedings of the British Academy*, p. 455.

2. "Criteria, Defeasibility, and Knowledge," revised and reprinted in *Perceptual Knowledge*, p. 209.

3. What I will focus on here is the incoherence of McDowell's proposed alternative to the view that criteria are defeasible. For a criticism of McDowell's argument against the possibility of knowledge based on defeasible criteria, see Paul Robinson's "McDowell Against Criterial Knowledge" (*Ratio* 4 [1991]). Robinson argues that McDowell's case against criterial knowledge turns on his denying that one can know that p even though one's basis for believing that p is compatible with not p. That is, McDowell is committed to the principle that "experiential knowledge cannot be constituted, even in part, by facts which are not required to obtain if the experience on which the knowledge claim is based is to be enjoyed. For in McDowell's view, someone could not be said to know that some x which was G was F on the basis of the generalization x(G→F) since he might be confronting some particular x which was G and not F.

4. Indeed, this is the first thing McDowell says in the revised edition of "Criteria, Defeasibility, and Knowledge." He writes, "One can sometimes know what someone else feels ... by ... what he says and does. It is very common for philosophers to interpret this idea so that 'what he says and does' is taken to allude to a basis for knowledge of what the person feels or thinks. Their thought of a basis has two elements. The first is that the basis is something knowable in its own right. . . . I argue that . . . the defeasibility of the inferential relation . . . is necessitated by the first of the two elements mentioned above" (p. 209).

5. As Robinson argues, McDowell owes us an argument for the principle that one cannot be said to know something is the basis upon which one claims to know it is compatible with the falsity of what one claims to know. And Canfield makes a similar point in *Wittgenstein: Language and World* (p. 122); he writes, "It is ... consistent to know something on a basis and yet for it to be logically possible for that thing to be false and the basis be true." I think that what Robinson and Canfield must mean or at any rate what they ought to say is that it is consistent to say that one is *correct* in saying that one knows something if one is justified in saying so, even if one turns out to be mistaken. For, as Canfield himself has said in conversation, it is part of the grammar of knowledge that knowledge entails the truth of what is known. Therefore, a case in which one turns out to be mistaken about what one has made a justified claim

to know is a case in which one was correct to say "I know" only before one's justification was lost. It is not a case in which one *knew*.

6. See Robinson, "McDowell Against Criterial Knowledge," p. 75.

7. For a similar argument against McDowell to the effect that "the world does not provide us with reasons," see Peter Baumann's "John McDowell: Mind and World," *Philosophische Rundschau* 44 (1997). According to Baumann, "[McDowell] proposes a 'rationalist' conception of mental content according to which thoughts can only have content if they entertain a rational (justificatory) relationship to the world. McDowell doesn't offer arguments for this claim. There are good reasons to doubt that thoughts and beliefs can be justified by something different from (other) thoughts and beliefs. McDowell often says that the world ("how things are," "things being thus and so") stands in a justificatory relation to our thoughts and beliefs (25, 112, 142 ff.). Davidson and many others would object that it is hard to see how the world could offer us reasons for our beliefs and thoughts."

8. McDowell may not be one of them. At least his argument in "Criteria, Defeasibility, and Knowledge" would be consistent with this. But the arguments against attributing knowledge and belief to nonlanguage users are powerful enough to make such attributions extremely contentious. As Davidson argues in "Rational Animals" (*Dialectica* 36 [1982]), in order to attribute to the dog the belief that the cat went up the oldest tree on the block or the oak tree, one would have to be justified in attributing to the dog the concepts of "tree" and "oak" and "oldest." And as Shanker points out in "The Conflict between Wittgenstein and Quine on the Nature of Language and Cognition and Its Implications for Constraint Theory," (p. 235), we cannot say that the dog has the concept of "mealtime" because he salivates to the sound of a bell. And this is not because we lack sufficient evidence to know what the dog is thinking but because the language game played with time demands far greater behavioral complexity than has been displayed by the dog in order to ascribe to it even a primitive version of that concept.

9. For a good defense of this view, see Canfield's " 'I Know I am in Pain' Is Senseless" in *Analysis and Metaphysics*, ed. Keith Lehrer (Dordrecht: Kluwer Academic Publishers, 1975) and Newton Garver's "Neither Knowing nor Not Knowing," *Philosophical Investigations* 7 (1984).

10. See P. M. S. Hacker's *Insight and Illusion: Themes in the Philosophy of Wittgenstein* (Oxford: Clarendon, 1986), p. 313.

11. It may seem, at first glance, as though McDowell's view is the same as Canfield's view. McDowell thinks that in successful pretense, the criteria for a pain ascription seem to be satisfied but are not really satisfied. And Canfield thinks that it is possible for us to mistakenly believe that the criterion of a claim is met. However, there is an enormous difference between McDowell's conception of what it is for a criterion of a claim to be satisfied and Canfield's conception of what it is for the criterion of a claim to be met. On Canfield's view, the criterion for saying that someone is in pain is met if that person exhibits the pain behavior which we treat as indicating pain and if the circumstances are

appropriate for us to apply our criterial rule. In other words, on Canfield's view, our *criterion* for saying "He is in pain" is a *basis* on which we judge that someone is in pain—a basis which is distinct from the pain itself but which indicates the presence of pain. Unlike McDowell, Canfield would not want to identify the criterion of some circumstance with the circumstance itself.

12. J. L. Martin, "A Dialogue on Criteria," *Philosophical Forum* 4 (1972), pp. 218–19.


## 10. Why Criteria Are Not Defeasible

1. As we shall see, Canfield (1981) challenges the assumption that we make judgments about whether others are in pain solely on the basis of their pain behavior. For a discussion of whether *P.I.* #580 suggests that criteria define mental processes or merely show that they have occurred, see John Hunter's "Wittgenstein on Inner Processes and Outer Criteria," *Canadian Journal of Philosophy* 7 (1977).

2. Canfield distinguishes between three different versions of the noninductive evidence view which I shall not discuss separately. For an independent treatment of each of them, see *Wittgenstein: Language and World*, pp. 79–95.

3. Sidney Shoemaker, *Self-Knowledge and Identity* (Ithaca: Cornell University Press, 1963), p. 4.

4. C. S. Chihara and J. A. Fodor, "Operationalism and Ordinary Language: A Critique of Wittgenstein," *American Philosophical Quarterly* 2 (1965), p. 286.

5. W. G. Lycan, "Noninductive Evidence: Recent Work on Wittgenstein's 'Criteria,' " *American Philosophical Quarterly* 8 (1971), p. 110.

6. Alvin Plantinga, *God and Other Minds* (Ithaca: Cornell University Press, 1967), p. 225.

7. Lycan, "Noninductive Evidence," p. 110.

8. Hacker, *Insight and Illusion* (Oxford: Clarendon, 1972), p. 153.

9. J. T. Richardson, *The Grammar of Justification* (New York: Palgrave, 1976), p. 122.

10. Canfield, *Wittgenstein: Language and World*, pp. 108–9.

11. Norman Malcolm makes this point in "Wittgenstein's Philosophical Investigations," reprinted in *Ludwig Wittgenstein: The Man and his Philosophy*, ed. K. T. Fann (New York: Prometheus Books, 1967), p. 200.

12. On the other hand, Carol Caraway gives an account of criteria which does take the importance of circumstances into account and she nevertheless maintains that we judge others to be in pain on the basis of defeasible criteria (see her "Criteria and Circumstances" in *Southern Journal of Philosophy* 22 [1984]). I do not think that this view is correct, although she makes a plausible case for it.

13. Those who make this inference include Gordon Baker ("Criteria: A New Foundation for Semantics," *Ratio* 16 [1974]), Richardson (1976), and Caraway (1984).

14. Canfield points this out in "Criteria and Rules of Language," *Philosophical Review* 83 (1974), p. 82.

15. Canfield (1981, p. 37) makes this point.

16. Lycan, "Noninductive Evidence," p. 109.

17. Canfield, "Criteria and Rules of Language," p. 82.

18. Canfield discusses this distinction in *Wittgenstein: Language and World* (1981), pp. 61–63.

19. See Canfield (1981), pp. 96–123.

20. See Canfield (1981), p. 116.

21. I owe this discussion to Canfield (1981), pp. 90–95, 123.

22. Canfield (1981), p. 91.

23. Canfield (1981), pp. 108, 114.

24. Canfield (1981), pp. 108–9.

25. Malcolm, "Wittgenstein's *Philosophical Investigations*," p. 200.

26. Hilary Putnam, "Brains and Behavior" in *Analytic Philosophy, Second Series*, ed. R. J. Butler (New York: Barnes and Noble, 1965), pp. 1–19.

27. I owe this discussion of Putnam to Canfield (1981), pp. 123–27.

28. Canfield (1981), p. 94.

## 11. Criterial Change, Conceptual Change, and Their Implications for the Concept of Truth

1. See Norman Malcolm's *Dreaming* (London: Routledge and Kegan Paul, 1957); Robert Hollinger's "Natural Kinds," *The Personalist* 55 (1974); Carol Caraway's "Criteria and Conceptual Change in Wittgenstein's Later Philosophy," *Metaphilosophy* 17 (1986), and Anthony Kenny's "Criterion," in *Encyclopedia of Philosophy*, ed. Paul Edwards (New York: Macmillan, 1967).

2. Newton Garver, "Wittgenstein on Criteria," in *Knowledge and Experience*, ed. C. D. Rollins (Pittsburgh: Pittsburgh University Press, 1962), p. 59.

3. Hans-Johann Glock, "Necessity and Normativity," in *The Cambridge Companion to Wittgenstein*, ed. David Stern and Hans Sluga (Cambridge, England: Cambridge University Press, 1996), p. 208.

4. Kripke, *Rules and Private Language*, p. 97.

5. Thus, Kripke remarks, "Wittgenstein proposes a picture of language based not on truth conditions but on assertibility conditions or justification conditions: under what circumstances are we allowed to make a given assertion" (1982), p. 74.

6. In "Meaning and Knowledge: The Place of Criteria in Epistemology" (*Dialectics and Humanism* 8 [1981]), Timo Airaksinen argues that the semantic aspect is more fundamental to criteria than the epistemological aspect. One argument he gives in support of the view that a criterion is a semantic concept rather than an epistemological one is that in the seventeenth century, witch-hunters who used the trial by water believed that they had evidence or criteria of illusory entities. However, in "Science and Certainty" (*Acta Philosophica Fennica*

32 [1981]), Lars Herzberg argues that people in the seventeenth century made an error in applying the word "witch" or that they should have used a different set of criteria. What we really want to say is that they should not have talked about witches at all or regarded certain phenomena as expressive of witchcraft. But to say this is to express a verdict on their way of life and that way of life was the frame of reference within which they made judgments.

7. Malcolm, *Dreaming*, p. 55.

8. William Dement and Nathaniel Kleitman, "The Relation of Eye Movements during Sleep to Dream Activity: An Objective Method for the Study of Dreaming," *Journal of Experimental Psychology* 53 (1957), p. 339.

9. Malcolm, *Dreaming*, p. 80.

10. Malcolm, *Dreaming*, p. 79–80.

11. Malcom, *Dreaming*, pp. 81–82.

12. Hilary Putnam, "Dreaming and Depth Grammar," *Analytic Philosophy, First Series*, ed. R. J. Butler (Oxford: Basil Blackwell, 1962), pp. 218–21.

13. Putnam, "Dreaming and Depth Grammar," pp. 220–21.

14. Putnam, *Representation and Reality* (Cambridge, Mass.: MIT Press, 1988), p. 11.

15. Putnam, "Dreaming and Depth Grammar," pp. 218–21.

16. See Lars Herzberg's "Criteria and the Philosophy of Science" (*Acta Philosophica Fennica* 30 [1978]), and Glock's "Necessity and Normativity" (1966).

17. Janna Thompson, "About Criteria," p. 37.

18. I owe this discussion to Herzberg's "Criteria and the Philosophy of Science," p. 43. Richard Rorty, in "Criteria and Necessity," *Nous* 7 (1973), argues that we need not suppose that criteria must be shared: all we need to suppose is that for every speaker there is some consideration that *he* holds to be decisive. But, as Herzberg points out, this sounds rather like arguing that we do not need shared rules to play soccer; it is enough that everyone plays by *some* rules.

19. I owe the preceding discussion to Glock's "Necessity and Normativity," pp. 211–12.

20. Glock, "Necessity and Normativity," p. 212.

21. Canfield makes this point in "Criteria and Method," p. 306, in which he criticizes Garver for saying that all statements which are treated as being true or false are governed by criteria.

22. Caraway, "Criteria and Conceptual Change in Wittgenstein's Later Philosophy," p. 166.

23. Michael Kober makes this remark in "Certainties of a World Picture: The Epistemological Investigations of *On Certainty*" in *The Cambridge Companion to Wittgenstein* ed. David Stern and Hans Sluga (Cambridge, England: Cambridge University Press, 1996), p. 428.

24. Canfield, *Wittgenstein: Language and World* (Amherst: University of Massachusetts Press, 1981), p. 38.

25. See also Caraway, "Criteria and Conceptual Change in Wittgenstein's Later Philosophy."

26. This is why, as Cora Diamond points out in "How Old are these Bones?" (*Aristotelian Society: Supplementary Volume*, 1999), we are willing to translate a word, as it was used before our criterion of it changed, as having meant the same as our present-day English word in cases where life with the word was more similar to ours than it was different.

27. See Canfield, *Wittgenstein: Language and World*, pp. 70–78.

28. Janna Thompson, "About Criteria."

29. Caraway ("Criteria and Conceptual Change in Wittgenstein's Later Philosophy," reads *Z.* #438 this way. However, she does not quote or discuss the entire passage.

30. I owe this discussion to Herzberg's "Criteria and Philosophy of Science," pp. 47–48.

31. Compare Peirce's remark, "What! Do you mean to say that what a man does not doubt is *ipso facto* true? . . . 'No, but . . . he has to regard what he does not doubt as absolutely true'" (*CP* 4. 416, 1905). Elsewhere, Peirce writes, "that which you do not at all doubt, you must and do regard as infallible, absolute truth" (*CP* 5. 416, 1905). However, since Peirce holds that the predicate "is true" gets applied fallibly, the last remark amounts to an equivocation on "infallible." One great advantage of the Wittgensteinian view of truth over the Peircean view is that the Wittgensteinian allows for a distinction between defeasibility and revisability. Therefore, the Wittgensteinian can help herself to Peirce's critical commonsensism without having to commit this type of equivocation on "infallible."

32. Judith Genova, in *Wittgenstein: A Way of Seeing*, p. 89, reads this passage as an argument that we should revise our concept of knowledge as guaranteeing truth. This may seem like a plausible reading, but I do not think that this is Wittgenstein's point here. What Wittgenstein says in this passage is not that I actually know that there's a chair there even when there isn't. What he says is that I can *say* that there's a chair there—or that I "have a right" to say this even when there isn't.

33. To understand this distinction, it must be kept in mind that the conditions under which it is correct to predicate "is true" of a sentence and the circumstances under which the sentence corresponds to reality can come apart.

34. For a good discussion of this, see Thomas Morawetz's "Understanding, Disagreement, and Conceptual Change."

35. See Lawrence Hinman's "Can a Form of Life Be Wrong?" p. 343.

## 12. Why a Revisionist Account of Truth?

1. Cheryl Misak has formulated the pragmatist view of truth in these three ways: as what would be believed at the end of inquiry, as what would be believed if inquiry were to be pursued as far as it could fruitfully go, and as what would best fit with evidence and argument. The latter is her considered opinion.

2. At this point, it is fair to say that there are certain objections that the Wittgensteinian and pragmatist can make against each other to which neither can reply without begging some questions. Nonetheless, the Wittgensteinian's position is stronger than the pragmatist's. All the pragmatist has to support her position is an appeal to a powerful and commonly held intuition. The Wittgensteinian has a good independent argument against snapping the link between meaning and agreement to support her opposing position.

3. Misak will reply that her inquirer might have alighted on a true belief and that further inquiry might continue to confirm it. But this reply surely invites the following question: Is her inquirer justified in inferring from the fact that further inquiry has continued to confirm her belief that her belief is *true*? Surely to say that she is justified in making this inference amounts to saying that she can really know that an inductive generalization is true. And the Peircean pragmatist would not want to say that we can know that an inductive generalization is true as distinct from saying that it is natural and rational to act *as though* it is true.

4. Dummett, *Truth and Other Enigmas*, p. 16. I have replaced Dummett's "Jones was brave" with "is true." The substitution makes a slightly different point, but it is also a point which Dummett would be happy to make.

# Bibliography

Addis, Mark. "Criteria: The State of the Debate." *Journal of Philosophical Research* 20 (1995).

Aireksinen, Timo. "Meaning and Knowledge: The Place of Criteria in Epistemology." *Dialectics and Humanism* 8 (1981).

Albritton, Rogers. "On Wittgenstein's Use of the Term 'Criterion.' " *Journal of Philosophy* 56 (1959).

Anscombe, G. E. M. "The Question of Linguistic Idealism." *Acta Philosophica Fennica* 28 (1976).

Arrington, Robert. "Criteria and Entailment." *Ratio* 21 (1979).

Austin, J. "Criteriology: A Minimally Correct Method." *Metaphilosophy* 10 (1979).

Baker, Gordon. "Criteria: A New Foundation for Semantics." *Ratio* 16 (1974).

————. *Language, Sense, and Nonsense.* Oxford: Blackwell, 1986.

Baumann, Peter. "John McDowell: *Mind and World*." *Philosophische Rundschau* 44 (1997).

Bennett, P. W. "Wittgenstein and Defining Criteria." *Philosophical Investigations* 1 (1978).

Berman, M. "Criteria and Defining Criteria in Wittgenstein." *International Logic Review* (1977).

Bienert, Ronald. "Wittgenstein's Concept of a Language Game." Ph.D. Diss. University of Toronto, 1996.

Bilgrami, Akeel. "Meaning, Holism, and Use." In *Truth and Interpretation: Perspectives on the Philosophy of Donald Davidson*, ed. Ernest Lepore. New York: Blackwell, 1986.

Blackburn, Simon. "Manifesting Realism." *Midwest Studies in Philosophy* 14 (1989).

Bloor, David. "The Question of Linguistic Idealism Revisited." In *The Cambridge Companion to Wittgenstein*, ed. Hans Stern and David Sluga. Cambridge, England: Cambridge University Press, 1996.

———. *Wittgenstein: A Social Theory of Knowledge.* London: Macmillan, 1983.

Bolton, Derek. "Life-Form and Idealism." In *Idealism, Past and Present*, ed. G. Vesey. Cambridge, England: Cambridge University Press, 1982.

Brandom, Robert. *Making It Explicit.* Cambridge, Mass.: Harvard University Press, 1995.

Canfield, John V. "Criteria and Method." *Metaphilosophy* 5 (1974).

———. "Criteria and Rules of Language." *Philosophical Review* 83 (1974).

———. " 'I Know I am in Pain' Is Nonsense." In *Analysis and Metaphysics*, ed. Keith Lehrer. Dordrecht: Kluwer Academic Publishers, 1975.

———. "The Living Language: Wittgenstein and the Empirical Study of Communication," *Language Sciences* 15 (1993).

———. *Wittgenstein: Language and World.* Amherst: University of Massachusetts Press, 1981.

———. "Wittgenstein versus Quine: The Passage into Language." In *Wittgenstein and Quine*, ed. Hans-Johann Glock and Robert L. Arrington. London: Routledge, 1996.

Caraway, Carol. "Criteria and Circumstances." *Southern Journal of Philosophy* 22 (1984).

———. "Criteria and Conceptual Change in Wittgenstein's Later Philosophy." *Metaphilosophy* 17 (1986).

———. "Is Wittgenstein's View of the Relation between Certainty and Knowledge Consistent?" *Philosophical Investigations* 1 (1978).

Chihara, C. S., and J. A. Fodor. "Operationalism and Ordinary Language: A Critique of Wittgenstein." *American Philosophical Quarterly* 2 (1965).

Clegg, J. "Symptoms." *Analysis* 32 (1972).

Cook, J. W. "Human Beings." In *Studies in the Philosophy of Wittgenstein,* ed. Peter Winch. London: Routledge and Kegan Paul, 1969.

Das Gupta. "Philosophy of Language: An Extended Epistemology (A Critique of Ordinary Language Philosophy and the Later Wittgenstein)." *International Philosophical Quarterly* 23 (1983).

Davidson, Donald. "Rational Animals." *Dialectica* 36 (1982).

———. "The Structure and Content of Truth." *Journal of Philosophy* 87 (1990).

Dement, William and Nathaniel Kleitman. "The Relation of Eye Movements During Sleep to Dream Activity: An Objective Method for the Study of Dreaming." *Journal of Experimental Psychology* 53 (1957).

Diamond, Cora. "How Old Are These Bones?" *Aristotelian Society Supplemental Volume* (1999).

Dummett, Michael. *Frege: Philosophy of Language.* London: Duckworth, 1973.

———. *Truth and Other Enigmas.* Cambridge, Mass.: Harvard University Press, 1978.

———. "The Metaphysics of Verificationism." In *The Philosophy of A. J. Ayer,* ed. L. Hahn. La Salle: Open Court, 1992.

———. "The Source of the Concept of Truth." In *Meaning and Method: Essays in Honour of Hilary Putnam* ed. G. Boolos. Cambridge, England: Cambridge University Press, 1990.

———. "What Is a Theory of Meaning I." In *Mind and Language: The Wolfson College Lectures,* ed. Samuel Guttenplan. Oxford: Clarendon 1974.

———. "What Is a Theory of Meaning II." In *Truth and Meaning,* ed. Gareth Evans and John McDowell. Oxford: Oxford University Press, 1976.

Ellenbogen, Sara. "On the Link between Frege's Platonic-Realist Semantics and his Doctrine of Private Senses." *Philosophy* 72 (1997).

Frege, Gottlob. "The Thought: A Logical Inquiry." In *Philosophical Logic,* ed. P. F. Strawson, translated by A. M. and Marcell Quinton. Oxford: Oxford University Press, 1964.

Garver, Newton. "Wittgenstein on Criteria." In *Knowledge and Experience: Proceedings of the Third Oberlin Colloquium in Philosophy*, ed. C. D. Rollins. Pittsburgh: Pittsburgh University Press, 1962.

———. "Neither Knowing Nor Not Knowing." *Philosophical Investigations* 7 (1984).

Genova, Judith. *Wittgenstein: A Way of Seeing*. New York: Routledge, 1995.

Gill, Jerry. "Wittgenstein's Concept of Truth." *International Philosophical Quarterly* 6 (1966).

Glock, Hans-Johann. "Necessity and Normativity." In *The Cambridge Companion to Wittgenstein*, ed. David Stern and Hans Sluga. Cambridge, England: Cambridge University Press, 1996.

———. "Truth Without People?" *Philosophy* 72 (1997).

Hacker, P. M. S. *Insight and Illusion: Wittgenstein on Philosophy and the Metaphysics of Experience*. Oxford: Clarendon, 1972.

———. *Insight and Illusion: Themes in the Philosophy of Wittgenstein*, revised second edition, Oxford: Clarendon, 1986.

———. *Scepticism, Rules, and Language*. Oxford: Blackwell, 1984.

———. *Wittgenstein, Rules, Grammar, and Necessity*. Oxford: Blackwell, 1984.

Hanfling, Oswald. *Wittgenstein's Later Philosophy*. Albany: State University of New York Press, 1989.

Hasker, William. "Theories, Analogies, and Criteria." *American Philosophical Quarterly* 8 (1971).

Herzberg, Lars. "Criteria and the Philosophy of Science." *Acta Philosophica Fennica* 30 (1978).

———. "Science and Certainty." *Acta Philosophica Fennica* 32 (1981).

Hinman, Laurence. "Can a Form of Life Be Wrong?" *Philosophy* 58 (1983).

Hollinger, Robert. "Natural Kinds." *The Personalist* 55 (1974).

Horwich, Paul. *Truth*. Oxford: Oxford University Press, 1998.

Hunter, John. "Wittgenstein on Inner Processes and Outer Criteria." *Canadian Journal of Philosophy* 7 (1977).

Kenny, Anthony. "Criterion." In *The Encyclopedia of Philosophy*, ed. Paul Edwards. New York: Macmillan, 1967.

Kirkham, Richard. "What Dummett Says about Truth and Linguistic Competence." *Mind* 98 (1989).

Kober, Michael. "Certainties of a World Picture: The Epistemological Investigations of *On Certainty*." In *The Cambridge Companion to Wittgenstein*, ed. David Stern and Hans Sluga. Cambridge, England: Cambridge University Press, 1996.

Koethe, J. L. "The Role of Criteria in Wittgenstein's Later Philosophy." *Canadian Journal of Philosophy* 7 (1977).

Kripke, Saul. *Wittgenstein on Rules and Private Language*. Cambridge, Mass.: Harvard University Press, 1982.

Loar, Brian. "Truth Beyond All Verificationism." In *Michael Dummett: Contributions to Philosophy*, ed. Barry M. Taylor. Dordrecht: Martinus Nijhoff, 1987.

Lycan, W. G. "Noninductive Evidence: Recent Work on Wittgenstein's 'Criteria.' " *American Philosophical Quarterly* 8 (1971).

Malcolm, Norman. *Dreaming*. London: Routledge and Kegan Paul, 1957.

———. "Wittgenstein's Philosophical Investigations" in *Ludwig Wittgenstein: The Man and His Philosophy*, ed. K. T. Fann. New York: Prometheus Books, 1967.

Martin, C. B. "Antirealism and the World's Undoing." *Pacific Philosophical Quarterly* 65 (1984).

Martin, J. L. "A Dialogue on Criteria." *Philosophical Forum* 4 (1972).

McDowell, John. "Antirealism and the Epistemology of Understanding." In *Meaning and Understanding*, ed. Herman Parret and Jacques Bouveresse. Berlin: W. deGruyter, 1981.

———. "Criteria, Defeasibility, and Knowledge." *Proceedings of the British Academy* 68 (1982).

———. "Criteria, Defeasibility, and Knowledge." Revised and reprinted in *Perceptual Knowledge*, ed. Jonathan Dancy. Oxford: Oxford University Press, 1988.

———. "Following a Rule." In *Wittgenstein: To Follow a Rule*, ed. Steven H. Holtzman and Christopher M. Leach. New York: Routledge and Kegan Paul, 1981.

———. "On 'The Reality of the Past.' " In *Action and Interpretation*, ed. Christopher Hookway and Philip Pettit. Cambridge, England: Cambridge University Press, 1978.

Misak, Cheryl. *Truth and the End of Inquiry: A Peircean Account of Truth.* Oxford: Clarendon, 1991.

———. *Verificationism: Its History and Prospects.* New York: Routledge, 1995.

Morawetz, Thomas. "Understanding, Disagreement, and Conceptual Change." *Philosophy and Phenomenological Research* 41 (1980).

Morick, Harold. "Do Wittgenstein and Quine Disagree About Certainty?" In *Language and Ontology,* ed. Jeffrey Leinfeller et al. Vienna: Hölder-Pichler-Tempsky, 1982.

Peirce, Charles Sanders. *Collected Papers of Charles Sanders Peirce.* Cambridge: Harvard University Press, 1958.

Plantinga, Alvin. *God and Other Minds.* Ithaca: Cornell University Press, 1967.

Polluck, J. L. "Criteria and Our Knowledge of the Material World." *Philosophical Review* 76 (1967).

Prawitz, Dag. "Dummett on a Theory of Meaning and Its Impact on Logic." In *Michael Dummett: Contributions to Philosophy,* ed. Barry M. Taylor. Dordrecht: Martinus Nijhoff, 1987.

Putnam, Hilary. "Brains and Behavior." In *Analytic Philosophy, Second Series,* ed. R. J. Butler. New York: Barnes and Noble, 1965.

———. "Dreaming and Depth Grammar." In *Analytic Philosophy, First Series,* ed. R. J. Butler. Oxford: Basil Blackwell, 1962.

———. *Reason, Truth, and History.* Cambridge, England: Cambridge University Press, 1981.

———. *Representation and Reality.* Cambridge, Mass.: MIT Press, 1988.

Quine, W. V. O. *Pursuit of Truth.* Cambridge, Mass.: Harvard University Press, 1990.

———. "Two Dogmas of Empiricism." In *From a Logical Point of View.* Cambridge, Mass.: Harvard University Press, 1953.

Richardson, J. T. *The Grammar of Justification.* New York: Palgrave, 1976.

Robinson, P. "McDowell Against Criterial Knowledge." *Ratio* 4 (1991).

Rorty, Richard. "Criteria and Necessity." *Nous* 7 (1973).

———. "Just One More Species Doing its Best." *London Review of Books* 25, no. 7 (1991).

————. "Representation, Social Practice, and Truth." *Philosophical Studies* 30 (1988).

Rosen, Gideon. "The Shoals of Language." *Mind* 104 (1995).

Rundle, B. *Wittgenstein and Contemporary Philosophy of Language.* Oxford: Blackwell, 1990.

Savigny, Ernst. "Some Doubts About Hopeless Dogs." In *The British Tradition in 20th Century Philosophy.* Vienna: Hölder-Pichler-Tempsky, 1995.

Schmitt, Frederick. *Truth: A Primer.* Boulder: Westview Press, 1995.

Scriven, M. "The Logic of Criteria." *Journal of Philosophy* 56 (1959).

Shanker, Stuart. *Wittgenstein and the Turning Point in Philosophy of Mathematics.* New York: State University of New York Press, 1987.

————. "The Conflict between Wittgenstein and Quine on the Nature of Language and Cognition and its Implications for Constraint Theory." In *Wittgenstein and Quine,* ed. Hans-Johann Glock and Robert L. Arrington. London: Routledge, 1996.

Shiner, Roger. "Canfield, Cavell, and Criteria." *Dialogue* 22 (1983).

Shoemaker, Sidney. *Self-Knowledge and Identity.* Ithaca: Cornell University Press, 1963.

Specht, Ernst. *The Foundations of Wittgenstein's Late Philosophy.* Manchester: Manchester University, 1969.

Sundholm, Goran. "Vestiges of Realism." In *The Philosophy of Michael Dummett,* ed. Brian McGuinness. Dordrecht: Kluwer Academic Publishers, 1994.

Temkin, J. "Wittgenstein on Criteria and Other Minds," *Southern Journal of Philosophy* 28 (1990).

Tenant, Neil. "Holism, Molecularity, and Truth." In *Michael Dummett: Contributions to Philosophy,* ed. Barry M. Taylor. Dordrecht: Martinus Nijhoff, 1987.

Thompson, Janna. "About Criteria." *Ratio* 13 (1971).

von Morstein, Petra. "Concepts and Forms of Life: Criteria and Perception." In *Wittgenstein, the Vienna Circle, and Critical Rationalism,* ed. H. Berghel et al. Vienna: Hölder-Pichler-Tempsky, 1979.

von Wright, G. H. "Wittgenstein on Certainty." In *Problems of the Theory of Knowledge,* ed. G. H. von Wright. The Hague: Martinus Nijhoff, 1972.

Waismann, F.. *The Principles of Linguistic Philosophy.* London: Macmillan, 1965.

Wellman, C. "Wittgenstein's Conception of a Criterion." *Philosophical Review* 71 (1962).

Winch, Peter. "True or False." *Inquiry* 31 (1986).

Winkler, Kenneth. "Scepticism and Antirealism." *Mind* 94 (1985).

Wittgenstein, Ludwig. The *Blue and Brown Books.* Oxford: Blackwell, 1958.

———. *On Certainty.* Edited by G. E. M. Anscombe and G. H. von Wright. Oxford: Basil Blackwell, 1961.

———. *Philosophical Grammar.* Ed. Rush Rhees, translated by Anthony Kenny. Oxford: Basil Blackwell, 1974.

———. *Philosophical Investigations.* Translated by G. E. M. Anscombe. Oxford: Blackwell, 1953.

———. *Philosophical Remarks.* Ed. Rush Rhees. Oxford: Blackwell, 1964.

———. *Zettel.* Edited by G. E. M. Anscombe and G. H. von Wright. Oxford: Blackwell, 1967.

Wolgast, E. H. "Certainty as a Form of Life." In *Philosophy of Mind— Philosophy of Psychology,* ed. Roderick Chisholm et al. Vienna: Hölder-Pichler-Tempsky, 1985.

———. "Wittgenstein and Criteria." *Inquiry* 7 (1964).

Wright, Crispin. *Frege's Conception of Numbers as Objects.* Aberdeen: Aberdeen University Press, 1983.

———. *Realism, Meaning, and Truth.* Oxford: Blackwell, 1987.

———. "Realism, Truth Value Links, Other Minds, and the Past." *Ratio* 22 (1980).

———. "Rule-following, Objectivity, and the Theory of Meaning." In *Wittgenstein: To Follow a Rule,* ed. Steven H. Notzman and Christopher M. Leach. New York: Routledge and Kegan Paul, 1981.

———. "Dummett and Revisionism." In *Michael Dummett: Contributions to Philosophy,* ed. Barry M. Taylor. Dordrecht: Martinus Nijhoff, 1987.

# Index

Made in the USA
Las Vegas, NV
15 March 2022

45674198R00095